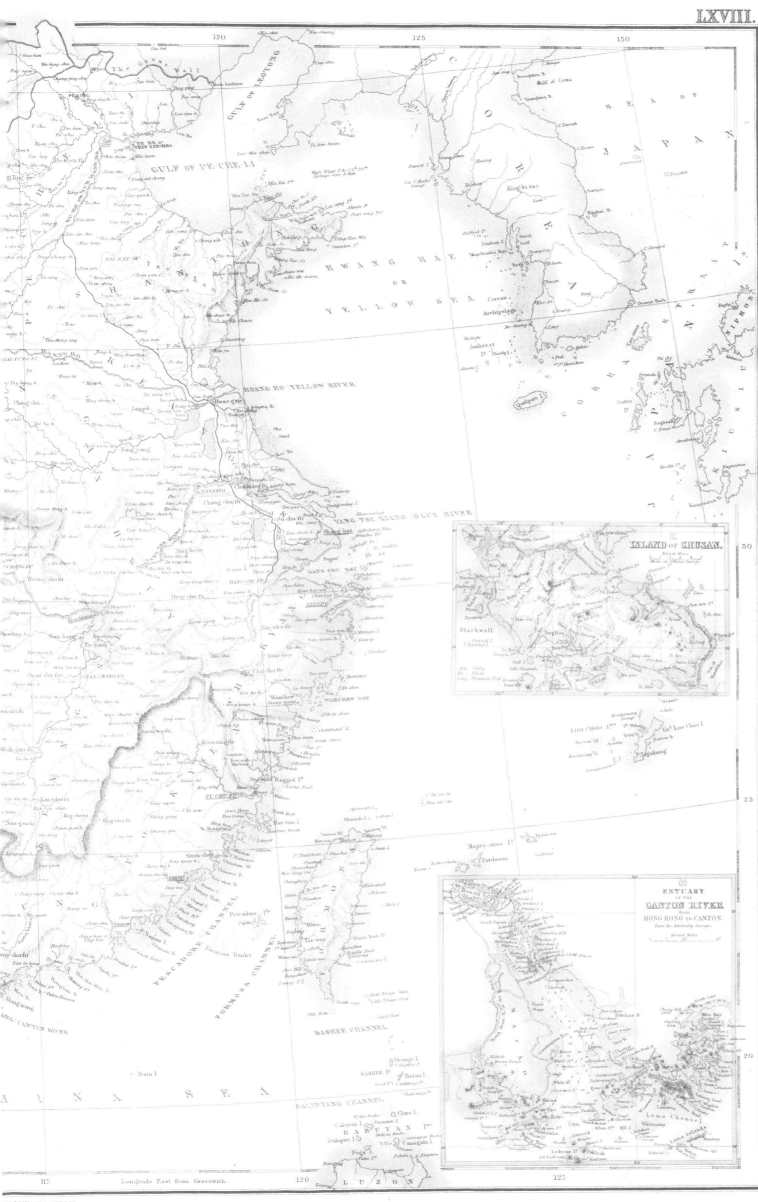

LEVENGER PRESS

First Edition 2009

Limited to 2,500 copies

This book is housed

in the library of

" Of Sericana, where Chineses drive
With sails and wind their cany waggons light."

Milton, Paradise Lost, Book III.

THE INMOST SHRINE

With grateful acknowledgment to

www.eastmanhouse.org

The Inmost Shrine

A Photographic Odyssey of China

1873

John Thomson

Foreword by Michael Meyer

Published by Levenger Press
420 South Congress Avenue
Delray Beach, Florida 33445 USA
Levengerpress.com

Originally published in 1873 by Sampson Low, Marston, Low, and Searle, London under the title *Illustrations of China and Its People.*

This Levenger Press edition contains Volume I of the four-volume original.

The 1872 map of China on the endpapers is reprinted with the kind permission of the David Rumsey Map Collection, www.davidrumsey.com.

Library of Congress Cataloging-in-Publication Data

Thomson, J. (John), 1837-1921.
  [Illustrations of China and its people. Vol. 1]
  The inmost shrine : a photographic odyssey of China, 1873 / John Thomson ;
foreword by Michael Meyer.
      p. cm.
  Originally published: London : Sampson Low, Marston, Low, and Searle, 1873
under the title Illustrations of China and its people, Vol. 1. With a new foreword.
  ISBN 978-1-929154-38-8
  1. China--Pictorial works. I. Meyer, Michael J., 1972- II. Title.
  DS709.T4752 2009
  951'.035--dc22
                            2009026002

Printed in the USA

Cover and book design by Danielle Furci
Mim Harrison, Editor

CONTENTS.

A GLIMPSE OF THE
GREAT MIDDLE KINGDOM

FOREWORD TO THE LEVENGER PRESS EDITION.

FOR his art, John Thomson was born at precisely the right time. The Edinburgh photographer's 1837 birth coincided with a year of events that would shape his life's work: Victoria ascended to the British throne, *Oliver Twist* became a serial success, and the continued perfection of the daguerreotype process captured images on silver plates. With Britain's colonial empire stretching to the Far East, a public accustomed to reading about society's underbelly, and the invention of photography, Thomson's travels and documentary portraits of commoners, their homes, and possessions helped lay the foundations of photojournalism, which makes this volume of Chinese portraits both historically and artistically unprecedented. The prints that follow also show us how much China has transformed itself, and how in many ways it remains the "Great Middle Kingdom" of Thomson's visits during imperial times.

As his contemporary Matthew Brady was photographing the horrors of American Civil War battlefields, Thomson sailed in 1862 to Singapore to visit his older brother, also a photographer. What was to have been a sojourn stretched to a decade in Asia. Thomson journeyed throughout Malaya, Sumatra and India, taking pictures of village life. In Siam and Cambodia, kings sat for portraits for him. In 1866, Thomson made the world's first photographic expedition to Angkor Wat. After that, he was hooked. A brief return to England, to public and court acclaim, ended when Thomson set his sights again on the Far East, first with a short stay in Saigon, then to a home and studio in Britain's newest Asian colony, Hong Kong.

The island ("Fragrant Harbor" in Chinese) was wrested by the United Kingdom after the first Opium War (1839-42), which forcibly opened China's markets—drug trade included—and the establishment of "treaty ports," cities where Western merchants and missionaries were free to operate. This cataclysmic humiliation to the Chinese throne was followed by the Second Opium War (1856-60), when Anglo-French forces sacked numerous cities, including the imperial capital of Beijing. There Lord Elgin (whose father had removed the marbles of the Parthenon to England a generation earlier) ordered the two ornate Summer Palaces looted and burned. To this day, Chinese schoolchildren are told to hold rancor against the "wolf-hearted" British soldiers.

So imagine the reception Thomson received when stepping off a Hong Kong ferry and onto Chinese shores eight years after war's end in 1868, to embark on a four-thousand-mile journey across rustic China, toting an unwieldy wooden-legged camera, fragile glass plates and explosive chemicals that would be impossible to procure after he ran out. Often, his only accomplice was his faithful dog, Spot. Thomson, then thirty-one, a lanky Scotsman whose bushy sideburns stretched to his chin, visited regions whose inhabitants had never laid eyes on a "barbarian," as all Westerners were commonly appended, let alone a camera, which Chinese then believed to be "the foreigner's silent and mysterious instrument of destruction," as Thomson writes, that would suck the soul from its subject.

He was "stoned and roughly handled on more than one occasion," though the violence was largely confined to large cities, where "the wide-spread hatred of foreigners is most conspicuously displayed." China's countryside village clans and wars felt familiar to a Scot, however, and it was in the interior that Thomson "met with numerous tokens of kindness, and hospitality as genuine as could be shown to a stranger in any part of the world."

Thomson's discovery echoed my own, contemporary experience. In 1995, freshly graduated from university with a degree in Spanish, I joined the Peace Corps—and was sent to China. Aside from what I knew from media images, the country was a veil; not only did I not speak Chinese, I could not even use chopsticks. Chinese cities were not welcoming, and I wondered if I had made a mistake in coming. But then I arrived in the rural Sichuan town in the country's deep southwest to train teachers in English, and I knew I would stay. For two years, and more than a century after Thomson had traveled nearby, I experienced numerous tokens of kindness and hospitality as genuine as could be shown to a stranger in any part of the world.

I learned Chinese—and how to use chopsticks—and like Thomson, my trip to China kept extending, to over a peripatetic decade. For two years I lived in a courtyard home in Beijing without heat or plumbing (but with wireless Internet), shared by several families in a venerable neighborhood just south of Tiananmen Square and on the cusp of destruction. I later chronicled the story in the book *The Last Days of Old Beijing*.

The book includes photographs, as modern Chinese are no longer fearful of the "soul-sucking" camera, unless—as anywhere—the image could land them in trouble. The pictures of my neighbors and students were easy to gather. As the book tells the tale of the capital's eight-hundred-year-old history, however, I also wanted to include historic photographs. These were much harder to procure. Due to what Chinese often summarize as the "vicissitudes of history"—to say nothing of various political regimes and tastes—archives through the centuries have been lost, or never assembled at all. In imperial times, pre-People's Republic, to depict a commoner rather than royalty would have been anathema, and unworthy as trade or art. As the Beijing historian and photographer Zhang Jinqi recently told me, "When looking for photographs of old China, I discovered Chinese depicted palaces, gardens and princes. It is extremely rare to see everyday life through a Chinese person's eyes. Photos taken by foreigners give the best account of old traditions."

Neither Zhang nor I had heard of John Thomson. And yet his images are recognizable to anyone who has perused reprinted photos at a Chinese antiques market. The variety of his subjects is remarkable: he captured imperious military and ministers, depopulated urban landscapes, tranquil monasteries, simple dwellings, musical instruments, toilet kits, silk and brocade, tattered rags of clothing.

I am often asked by younger Chinese why they should care about old photographs or objects, and why Westerners seem to dote on these accouterments of their culture. In an era of prosperity, when everything can be renewed or made new, why look back, unless to exult at how far one's society has come? I agree: no one should live in poverty, no matter how picturesque. But the university students I taught while in the Peace Corps were assigned—like their peers nationwide—the novels of Dickens. Why, I asked them, read *Oliver Twist*, when London has changed so greatly?

Because like novelists, photojournalists such as Thomson seem preternaturally aware that recording the past instructs the present and future. In Vladimir Nabokov's short story "A Guide to Berlin," the narrator tells a friend about his trip to the aquarium. The bored listener finally interrupts and says none of it matters. "I can't understand what you see." The narrator fumes within: "How can I demonstrate to him that I have glimpsed somebody's future recollection?" Later the narrator contemplates such a remembrance:

> I think that here lies the sense of literary creation: to portray ordinary objects as
> they will be reflected in the kindly mirrors of future times; to find in the objects
> around us the fragrant tenderness that only posterity will discern and appreciate in
> far-off times when every trifle of our plain everyday life will become exquisite and
> festive in its own right: the times when a man who might put on the most ordinary
> jacket of today will be dressed up for an elegant masquerade.

And so here are China's people and objects, circa the 1860s, when China was a feudal society ruled by an emperor. Foot binding and opium are now forbidden, of course, but many of Thomson's subjects are recognizable today. The sedan chair has been resurrected for mountain travelers and brides. The long braided queue men had to wear by imperial decree is seen on barkers and souvenirs. Colonnaded structures built by British colonists have been turned into Communist Party offices or Starbucks. Urban women still "dread being tanned by the sun" (as mere laborers have bronzed skin) and nationwide, two strings "act as pincers" to remove hair from women's faces. Pawnshops have returned. Tea drinking is en vogue. "Schroffing"—the act of examining currency for validity—no longer has its own houses, but Chinese snap and stare at present-day bills, suspicious of counterfeits. Like the British in Hong Kong, the Portuguese have returned Chinese dominion to Macau, which has become a lusty port of Las Vegas-backed casinos.

Thomson's China travels took him from Guangzhou (Canton) north through Shanghai to Beijing, and through the Great Wall. After the four-year journey, he returned to London, publishing the photos in four volumes, of which this Levenger Press edition comprises the first. Thomson then gained further renown for his portraits of London's working poor, published in 1878 in a monthly magazine of his founding (and prefiguring Jacob Riis's study of New York City's tenements, *How the Other Half Lives*, which appeared in 1890).

And then, a turn: In 1881, Victoria, who became queen the year Thomson was born, appointed him as photographer of the royal family, a position he parlayed into a career shooting portraits of British high society and instructing the Royal Geographical Society on documenting its explorations. But the era of Rule Britannia in which Thomson rose was ending. The Great War that ended in 1918 was not the war to end them all, as proclaimed. In 1921, when Thomson turned eighty-four, anti-European riots broke out in Egypt, the Irish Free State was ratified, Adolph Hitler became fuehrer of the Nazi party, the Bolsheviks were a year from consolidating the Union of Soviet Socialist Republics, and the Chinese Communist Party was founded, prefiguring a seismic change in the nation that continues today.

The photographer and his camera were retired to his native Edinburgh. Upon his death in October 1921, the Royal Geographical Society named one of the peaks of Mount Kilimanjaro in his honor—Point Thomson. He had never been to Africa.

—*Michael Meyer*

INTRODUCTION BY THE AUTHOR.

Y design in the accompanying work is to present a series of pictures of China and its people, such as shall convey an accurate impression of the country I traversed as well as of the arts, usages, and manners which prevail in different provinces of the Empire. With this intention I made the camera the constant companion of my wanderings, and to it I am indebted for the faithful reproduction of the scenes I visited, and of the types of race with which I came into contact.

Those familiar with the Chinese and their deeply-rooted superstitions will readily understand that the carrying out of my task involved both difficulty and danger. In some places there were many who had never yet set eyes upon a pale-faced stranger ; and the literati, or educated classes, had fostered a notion amongst such as these, that, while evil spirits of every kind were carefully to be shunned, none ought to be so strictly avoided as the " Fan Qui " or " Foreign Devil," who assumed human shape, and appeared solely for the furtherance of his own interests, often owing the success of his undertakings to an ocular power, which enabled him to discover the hidden treasures of heaven and earth. I therefore frequently enjoyed the reputation of being a dangerous geomancer, and my camera was held to be a dark mysterious in-strument, which, combined with my naturally, or supernaturally, intensified eyesight gave me power to see through rocks and mountains, to pierce the very souls of the natives, and to produce mira-culous pictures by some black art, which at the same time bereft the individual depicted of so much of the principle of life as to render his death a certainty within a very short period of years.

Accounted, for these reasons, the forerunner of death, I found portraits of children difficult to obtain, while, strange as it may be thought in a land where filial piety is esteemed the highest of virtues, sons and daughters brought their aged parents to be placed before the foreigner's silent and mysterious instrument of destruction. The trifling sums that I paid for the privilege of taking such subjects would probably go to help in the purchase of a coffin, which, conveyed ceremoniously to the old man's house, would there be deposited to await the hour of dissolution, and the body of the parent whom his son had honoured with the gift. Let none of my readers suppose that I am speaking in jest. To such an extreme pitch has the notion of honouring ancestors with due mortuary rites been carried in China, that an affectionate parent would regard children who should present him with a cool and comfortable coffin as having begun in good time to display the duty and respect which every well-regulated son and daughter is expected to bestow.

The superstitious influences, such as I have described, rendered me a frequent object of mistrust, and led to my being stoned and roughly handled on more occasions than one. It is, however, in and about large cities that the wide-spread hatred of foreigners is most conspicuously displayed. In many of the country districts, and from officials who have been associated with Europeans, and who therefore appreciate the substantial benefits which foreign intercourse can confer, I have met with numerous tokens of kindness, and a hospitality as genuine as could be shown to a stranger in any part of the world.

It is a novel experiment to attempt to illustrate a book of travels with photographs, a few years back so perishable, and so difficult to reproduce. But the art is now so far advanced, that we can multiply the copies with the same facility, and print them with the same materials as in the case of woodcuts or engravings. I feel somewhat sanguine about the success of the under-taking, and I hope to see the process which I have thus applied adopted by other travellers; for the faithfulness of such pictures affords the nearest approach that can be made towards placing the reader actually before the scene which is represented.

The letter-press which accompanies the pictures, and which will render them, as I trust, more interesting and more intelligible, is compiled from information derived from the most trustworthy sources, as well as from notes either made by me at the time the subjects were taken, or gathered during a residence of nearly five years in China.

I have endeavoured to arrange these notes and illustrations as far as possible in the natural order or sequence of my journeys, which extended over a distance, estimated roughly, of between 4,000 and 5,000 miles.

I shall start from the British colony of Hong-Kong, once said to be the grave of Europeans, but which now, with its city of Victoria, its splendid public buildings, parks and gardens, its docks, factories, telegraphs and fleets of steamers, may be fairly considered the birthplace of a new era in eastern civilization. I will next proceed by the Pearl river to Canton, the city above all others possessing the greatest historical interest to foreigners, as the scene of their early efforts to gain a footing in the country. Thence I will cross to Formosa, an island which, by its tropical luxuriance and by the grandeur of its mountain scenery, deserves the name "Isla Formosa" which the early Portuguese voyagers conferred upon it. At Taiwan the ruin of the old fort Zelandia will be found both curious and interesting; it was the stronghold from which Koksinga, the famous Chinese adventurer, succeeded in driving the Dutch, some of whom are said to have sought shelter among the aborigines, who still possess old Dutch documents, and have traditions about the doings of their kind-hearted, red-haired brothers. This island is daily rising in importance, as the recent development of its resources is fostering a growing trade at the open ports, and it is destined to play a leading part in the future as one of the great coal-fields of China.

Crossing to the mainland, I will visit Swatow and Chow-chow-fu, noted for the quality of their sugar and rice, for their turbulent clans, and for village wars that remind one of the feudal times of Scotland.

I shall then pass northward to Amoy, one of the first ports visited by foreigners, remarkable in modern times as that part of the Fukien province from which a constant tide of emigration flows to the Straits of Malacca and to America, and noticeable also for the independent character of its people, as among the last who succumbed to the Tartar yoke. The river Min will here afford examples of the grand mountain scenery to be found in the Fukien province, and will form an attractive portion of the work, as the great artery which carries an annual supply of about seventy million pounds of tea to the Foochow market.

Following the route northward the reader will next be introduced to Shanghai, the greatest of the treaty ports of China, where, within a few years, a foreign settlement has sprung up, on the banks of the Woosang, of such vast proportions, as to lead a visitor to fancy that he has been suddenly transported to one of our great English ports; the crowd of shipping, the wharves, warehouses, and landing-stages, the stone embankment, the elegance and costliness of the buildings, the noise of constant traffic in the streets, the busy roads, smooth as a billiard-table, and the well-kept garden that skirts the river affording evidence of foreign taste and refinement, all tending to aid the illusion. One has only, however, to drive beyond the foreign settlement to dispel the dream, and to find the native dwellings huddled together, as if pressed back to make way for the higher civilization that has planted a city in their midst. Leaving Shanghai, I will proceed to Ningpo and Snowy Valley, the favourite spring resort of Shanghai residents, and justly celebrated for the beauty of its azaleas, its mountain scenery, its cascades and waterfalls; thence to the Yangtsze Kiang, visiting *en route* the treaty ports and the ancient capital, Nankin, passing through the weird scenery of the gorges of the Upper Yangtsze, and penetrating as far as Kwei-chow-fu. The concluding journey will embrace Chefoo, the Peiho, Tientsin and Peking. The remarkable antiquities, the palace, temples, and observatory; the different races in the great metropolis; the ruins of the Summer Palace and the Ming Tombs shall be presented to the reader: after which I will guide him through the Nankow Pass, and take my leave of him at the Great Wall.

2

LIST OF ILLUSTRATIONS.

LIST OF ILLUSTRATIONS.

PRINCE KUNG.

PRINCE KUNG, now about forty years of age, is the sixth son of the Emperor Tao Kwang, who reigned from A. D. 1820 to 1850. He is a younger brother of the late Emperor Hien-foong, and, consequently an uncle to the reigning Emperor Tung-che. Prior to 1860 he was little known beyond the precincts of the Court : but, when the Emperor fled from the summer palace, it was he who came forward to meet the Ministers of the Allied Powers, and negotiate the conditions of peace. He holds several high civil and military appointments, the most important that of member of the Supreme Council, a department of the Empire resembling most nearly the Cabinet with us. Quick of apprehension, open to advice, and comparatively liberal in his views, he is the acknowledged leader of that small division among Chinese politicians who are known as the party of progress.

Independently of his various offices, Prince Kung, as his title denotes, is a member of the highest order of Chinese nobility ; an expression which, to prevent misconception, we must beg our readers' permission to explain. There have been from the most ancient times in China five degrees of honour, to which men whose services have been eminent may attain ; the titles vesting, as we should say, in remainder to their heirs male. The latter, however, cannot succeed without revival of their patent, and even then, as a rule, the title they succeed to is one degree less honourable than that of their predecessor ; so that were the usage in vogue with us a dukedom would dwindle to a baronetcy in five generations.

The Manchu family, which rules the country, or to speak more correctly those of the stock who are within a certain degree of the Imperial line, have no less than eighteen orders of nobility, liable, however, like the old system spoken of above, to gradual extinction, except in a few particular instances where the patent ensures the title in perpetuity.

Prince Kung received such a patent in 1865.

I.

HONG-KONG.

ONG-KONG is one of a group of islands situated a little north of the mouth of the Canton or Pearl river. It is about ten miles long, by four and a-half in breadth, and of igneous formation. From east to west, along its entire length, there runs a central rocky ridge or spine, chiefly composed of granite, and broken up into a series of jagged peaks, whose greatest elevation is 1,900 feet. Viewed from a distance, Hong-Kong may be readily distinguished from the islands which surround it by the bold outlines, and superior altitude, of its hills. The contrast in many cases being as striking as that between the islands of Arran and Bute. The granite in some parts of the island is in a state of disintegration; but great masses of the solid stone are to be found, and have proved of service in the construction of the forts, the docks, and the city of Victoria. The latter is to the north of the island, on the slope of the hill named Victoria Peak, and faces that portion of the mainland which is known as British Kowloon. The Kowloon coast here, and the northern shore of Hong-Kong, combine to form one of the finest harbours in the world, having a space of over six miles in length by two in breadth, available for the safe anchorage of the largest ships. The view which fronts this page is taken from the residence of Messrs. Jardine, Matheson and Co. at East Point. In the immediate foreground is shown the entrance to Wong-nei-chong or Happy Valley, noted for its picturesque hill scenery, its race-course, and its cemetery for Europeans. The eminence to the left is Morrison's Hill, crowned with a row of substantially built foreign residences, and commanding an extensive and imposing view of the city and ports.

Victoria, with its long line of wharves and warehouses, its public buildings, and its private residences in elegant rows, is seen resting on the slope of the hill; while characteristic masses of fleecy cloud are wrapped around the peak above. The masts of the shipping, which rise like a forest about the Victoria promontory, may give the reader some conception of the magnitude of our trade at Hong-Kong. By the treaty of Nankin, in 1842, the island was ceded to the British, and was erected into a colony on the 5th of April, 1843.

Previous to the above dates Hong-Kong was as barren and uninteresting as the islands around it at the present day, where one can find nothing more than a few fishing hamlets, enjoying, however, a degree of prosperity unknown before the advent of the British flag. There is only one ancient privilege the loss of which these villagers, it may be, deplore. Those among them who wore the peaceful garb of fishermen used to vary their pursuits, a little more than twenty-five years ago, by engaging in piracy when opportunities occurred. So confirmed is their relish for buccaneering, that, in spite of the heavy penalties now imposed upon the crime, it has not yet been completely rooted out; and, although much rarer, we still hear of piratical outrages in or near the very harbour of Hong-Kong. Such notices as the following, not unfrequent during the early history of the colony, are happily seldom met with in the present day: —"In March, 1846, a large body of pirates, some eighty in number, plundered the village of Shek-pai-wan,"[1] now known to foreigners as Aberdeen, and boasting an extensive dock. "On the 25th of April, 1854, a severe encounter took place between the police and a gang of hill robbers at Shek-pai-wan, in which several of the robbers were shot."[2] "Twenty-two piracies are noted in Hong-Kong waters between the 1st November, 1856, and 15th January, 1857."[3]

On the 15th January, 1857, an attempt was made to poison the entire foreign community by the Chinese bakers, who introduced arsenic into the bread. Had the drug been admixed in smaller quantities, an awful catastrophe might have taken place. But the presence of the poison was so easily detected, that public criers, promptly sent round, were in time to prevent many from taking the bread. These bakers had, no doubt, been bribed by more influential parties; but we believe few, if any, of the offenders were punished for the crime. When to the foregoing calendar of horrors we add the malignant fever, which swept off foreigners by the score, due, as was supposed, to the noxious gases exhaled from the surfaces of decomposed granite laid bare during the erection of the city, we must admit that the island fairly earned its reputation as the grave of Europeans.

---

[1] "Treaty Ports of China and Japan," p. 60. [2] *Ibid.* p. 68. [3] *Ibid.* p. 73.

Both it and the native inhabitants have undergone marvellous changes within the last twenty-five years. A splendid town has been built out of its barren rocks; and the hill-sides are covered with trees, which not only enhance the picturesqueness of the place, but are of great value in purifying the air, and improving the health of the population. In morality, too, it has undergone a change; though perhaps not quite so marked, as the organization of the police has become more perfect, while the good feeling and interest of the wealthy and respectable class of native residents have been enlisted in the suppression of crime.

The bands of desperate ruffians that used to infest the island are fast disappearing, although Hong-Kong still holds its own in crimes below piracy and assassination. The terrors of the law are insufficient to suppress pilfering and petty larceny, practised among domestic and other servants; and perjury constantly recurs, as the lower ranks of natives deem it fully as meritorious to benefit their friends by swearing to a lie as it would be criminal to injure them by telling the truth on oath. Under British rule, the population of Hong-Kong had increased from 7,450 in 1841, to 125,504, as returned by the census of 1865.[1] The resident foreign community is estimated at over 2,000, principally Europeans and Americans; few, if any, having been born at the place. The majority of these men are engaged in trade, and only reside in Hong-Kong long enough to obtain a competency with which they may retire to their native land. The facilities of transit now afforded by the various lines of steamers render a trip home so inexpensive and expeditious, that those who can afford it frequently avail themselves of a run to the old country; the more so as the increased commercial activity and competition of the present day have lengthened indefinitely the period of residence necessary for the accumulation of even a modest fortune.

"Treaty Ports of China and Japan," p. 17.

II.

HONG-KONG HARBOUR.

N this view, taken when H. R. H. the Duke of Edinburgh visited Hong-kong in 1869, H. M. S. Galatea is seen at anchor off Peddar's Wharf. Those familiar with the place will readily recognize the well-known range of hills that shelters the harbour on the Kowloon side; and few who were present when the Duke was landing will forget the scene that was then presented in the harbour. Ships of all nations vied in the splendour of their decorations; long lines of merchant boats guarded the approach to the wharf; and on a thousand native crafts, adorned with flags and shreds of gaudy cloth, appeared the dusky multitudes of the floating population, swarming over the decks, or clinging to the rigging of their vessels. The wharves too, and landing stages, were covered with a sea of yellow faces, all eager to catch a glimpse of the great English prince. Nor can I forget the regret expressed by some at finding that he was only a man after all, attired in the simple uniform of a captain; with no display of purple and fine linen, and with none of the mystic emblems of royalty to hedge his dignity around. A very different being this, surely, from the offspring of their own great Emperor, who is brother of the sun, and kinsman to the moon, on whose radiant countenance no common mortal can look and live.

The harbour, although sheltered by the hills of the mainland and Hong-kong, as well as by the islands round about, often suffers from the violence of the typhoons which are common during winter to the China seas.

During the typhoon months, the floating population, which numbers about 30,000 souls, carefully study the indications of the weather, and can calculate with great shrewdness the near approach of a storm. They usually, however, verify their own observations by ascertaining the barometrical changes from the foreign ship-captains in port. When they have settled in their own minds that a storm is coming on, the boats and fishing population cross the harbour " en masse," and shelter in the bays of Kowloon until the fury of the hurricane is spent. Round the harbour the scenery is remarkably picturesque, and picnic parties during the cold season find many a pleasant retreat among the islands, particularly Green Island and Wong-chuen-chow, or amid the woody hills and fertile valleys which diversify the mainland of Kowloon.

III.

A HONG-KONG SEDAN CHAIR.

HERE are no cabs in Hong-Kong; sedan chairs are the only public conveyances. The newly-arrived resident seldom takes kindly to this substitute for the wheeled vehicles of home, and is for a time affected with a sentiment of compassion towards the unfortunate men who bear him about on their shoulders. This, however, soon wears off: he feels the necessity of rest after a hard day's work in a hot, trying climate, and marks the happy, contented faces of the sturdy chair-bearers who clamour, all unconscious of degradation, for the favour of his regular patronage, and for the trifle which is to be paid for his fare. Chair-stands are to be found at all the hotels, at the corners of the chief thoroughfares, as well as on the wharves, where the eager chair-coolies pounce upon each freshly-arrived stranger as he lands at the port. These bearers vie with each other in keeping their chairs clean and attractive-looking, and in displaying to advantage the muscular proportions of their well-formed limbs, never weary of climbing the steep and. tortuous streets, or the scorching pathways that wind about the hill. They address all sailors by the familiar cognomen of "Jack," while strangers in more costly attire come under the designation of "Captain." Simple are the habits of these chair-coolies! During the greater part of the year they have no settled dwelling, and sleep in the open air, at some spot where they will wake to find business early astir. They find their food cooked and ready at the street stalls, and they easily procure substitutes when they wish a few days' leisure and enjoyment.

Public chairs are licensed, and each carries a printed tariff of charges exposed in the chair, ranging from ten cents for the lowest fare to two dollars for the day. Sedan chairs have been in use in China from ancient times, and at the present day, in all parts of the country, they are looked upon as an important article in a civil officer's equipment, the rank of the owner being indicated by the number of bearers and followers attached to his sedan. Military officers are not permitted to employ chairs; if they do not care to walk, they are at liberty to use horses.

In some parts of the interior, as, for example, in the mountainous country above Ningpo, chairs of a lighter build are used for the ascent of the hills; these consist of a simple seat of ratan fixed to two bamboo poles, and having a narrow board slung from the chair by two cords for the purpose of resting the feet.

The chair of most importance is the Bridal chair. It is richly ornamented and gilded, and is hung with red silk curtains, which screen the blushing fair one, on the day of marriage, from the intrusive vulgar gaze. These Bridal chairs, as well as the gaudy paraphernalia suitable for the occasion, are hired from a contractor.

A CHINESE SCHOOL-BOY.

GOVERNMENT Schools for the education of native boys have long been established in different parts of Hong-Kong, and, in conjunction with the schools of the various Christian missions, contain about 2,000 boys, who receive an ordinary English education, such as fits them for useful employment as interpreters, compradores, treasurers, or clerks. The position these educated Chinamen fill in our official and commercial establishments could not well be undertaken by Europeans, for the Chinaman possesses a knowledge of the language and habits of his countrymen which a foreigner can never acquire, while his acquaintance with English is rarely sufficient to raise him above the status of a very careful painstaking copying clerk or accountant; although, versed as he is in our method of accounts, and quite at home in the equally perfect system of his own country, he proves in our mercantile offices a most valuable acquisition.

I have heard the industry and aptitude of the Chinese school-boy highly praised by those who have had experience in teaching European children and natives of the country side by side; and I am assured that, notwithstanding the obvious disadvantages under which the native labours in having to acquire a foreign language and foreign habits of thought, his capacity for learning is so great that it will sustain him neck and neck in the race with his European rival.

There are a number of schools in different parts of the country, supported by the Chinese Government, in which foreign languages and sciences are taught by foreign and native professors. The most important, probably, is the College at Peking, under the supervision of Dr. Martin. There is also an extensive training-school at Foochow, where the pupils are taught naval architecture, engineering, mechanics, and the science of navigation. In this school the theoretical training is reduced to practice in the construction of steamers on the most approved foreign models, and by employment in actual navigation.

A CHINESE GIRL.

THE education of the girls of a Chinese family is conducted within the domestic circle. They are strictly secluded, and consequently Chinese history offers few examples of women who have been distinguished for their literary attainments. In the higher orders of society ladies here and there receive an education which enables them to form some slight acquaintance with the literature of their country, and to conduct and express themselves according to the strict and formal rules of etiquette which pertain to their position as the daughters or wives of men of learning and cultivation. In a few cases they are taught elegant accomplishments, playing on the lute, for example, that they may charm the leisure hours of their lords with song, but the science to which they devote themselves with most assiduity is the knowledge of the mysteries of cosmetics and the toilet; how to paint to the proper tint, finishing with the bright vermilion spot on the under lip; how to poise the quivering ornaments of kingfisher plumes or sprays of pearls about the coiffure; how to walk with grace on their tiny feet, and to sit down without furling or disarranging a fold of their silken attire. The women of the lower classes are seldom taught anything beyond the duties of the household, or the more arduous work of bearing burdens or labouring with the men of their family in the fields. Tea-picking, and the rearing of the silk-worm, are also female occupations. Such an education as this, however, is not unsuited for their lowly station in life, as they are trained to strict habits of industry and domestic economy.

A HONG-KONG ARTIST.

LUMQUA was a Chinese pupil of Chinnery, a noted foreign artist, who died at Macao in 1852. Lumqua produced a number of excellent works in oil, which are still copied by the painters in Hong-Kong and Canton. Had he lived in any other country he would have been the founder of a school of painting. In China his followers have failed to grasp the spirit of his art. They drudge with imitative servile toil, copying Lumqua's or Chinnery's pieces, or anything, no matter what, just because it has to be finished and paid for within a given time, and at so much a square foot. There are a number of painters established in Hong-Kong, but they all do the same class of work, and have about the same tariff of prices, regulated according to the dimensions of the canvas. The occupation of these limners consists mainly in making enlarged copies of photographs. Each house employs a touter, who scours the shipping in the harbour with samples of the work, and finds many ready customers among the foreign sailors. These bargain to have Mary or Susan painted on as large a scale and at as small a price as possible, the work to be delivered framed and ready for sea probably within twenty-four hours. The painters divide their labour on the following plan. The apprentice confines himself to bodies and hands, while the master executes the physiognomy, and thus the work is got through with wonderful speed. Attractive colours are freely used; so that Jack's fair ideal appears at times in a sky-blue dress, over which a massive gold chain and other articles of jewellery are liberally hung. These pictures would be fair works of art were the drawing good, and the brilliant colours properly arranged; but all the distortions of badly taken photographs are faithfully reproduced on an enlarged scale. The best works these painters do are pictures of native and foreign ships, which are wonderfully drawn. To enlarge a picture they draw squares over their canvas corresponding to the smaller squares into which they divide the picture to be copied. The miniature painters in Hong-Kong, and Canton do some work on ivory that is as fine as the best ivory painting to be found among the natives of India, and fit to bear comparison with the old miniature painting of our own country, which photography has, now-a-days, in a great measure superseded.

I shall have occasion to notice Chinese art and artists in a subsequent portion of this work.

IV.

IV.

IV.

IV.

THE CLOCK-TOWER, HONG-KONG.

THE clock-tower, designed by Mr. Rawlings in 1861, is a great ornament to the city, the clock too, when regulated properly, is of no inconsiderable service. It has, however, been a victim to the climate, and is liable to fits of indisposition, resting from its duties at the most inconvenient seasons, as if unable to contend against the heat. The tower is seen to advantage from the harbour, and the lighted dial of the clock forms a good landmark to guide the benighted steersman to the landing steps at Pedders wharf. In the street which conducts to the clock-tower from the wharf stand several of the oldest buildings in the Colony. On the right of this picture we see the residence lately occupied by Messrs. Hunt and Co.

In the foreground, to the left, is shown a part of the west wing of the palatial-looking building erected by Messrs. Dent, when commerce was most flourishing in the settlement; this edifice is now tenanted by three separate mercantile houses. On the left, and nearest to the tower, stands the Hong-Kong Hotel, constructed after the model of the large hotels in London. It has not proved to the shareholders a very profitable undertaking, being on a scale too vast for the requirements of the place. At present it is rented and conducted by a Chinaman, and none but Chinese cooks and waiters are employed. The management is good, and the hotel comfortable. To a visitor the large dining hall presents an animated and interesting scene, and he finds on further experience that the arrangements are perfect and the fare unexceptionable. The native waiters are remarkable no less for promptitude and politeness, than for the spotless purity of their light silk or linen robes, and for the fluency of " Pidgin " English, in which they converse; this is, however, a jargon intelligible only to the residents. The younger boy-servitors pronounce with a pure English accent; they can also read, write, and reckon in our language with facility, having most of them been trained at the Government School.

The turbaned figure on the right is an Indian policeman, of whom there were at one time about 300 in the force. They are now being gradually drafted off to India, and replaced by Europeans and West-Indian negroes. These tall Indian members of the constabulary were admitted on all hands to be highly ornamental, but proved comparatively useless for the maintenance of order among the Chinese, as, with one or two notable exceptions, they could neither converse in English nor in the language of China. One or two of the chair coolies are seen waiting for a fare; and as these men perform very important services for the native and foreign community, I propose to furnish the reader with a more detailed account of them on another page.

V.

THE PRAYA, HONG-KONG.

 HE Praya (for so the Portuguese term the broad stone-faced road along the harbour in front of the city) affords a pleasant drive some miles in extent, and joins the route to Show-ke-wan in the Ly-ee-moon Pass through which we approach the port from the East. This view is taken from the front of the Parade ground, and represents the principal business part of the Praya. The block of buildings facing the water on the left are the premises of the Hong-Kong and Shanghai and Chartered Mercantile Banks. The huge edifice in the centre was erected by Messrs. Dent. The merchants commonly have their offices on the ground-floor, and reside in the chambers above; there they command an extensive view of the harbour as they promenade in spacious verandahs " when the wind bloweth in from the sea."

The architecture is massive and strong, yet the designer has managed to impart an appearance of lightness to his work, insufficient, one would fancy, to resist the typhoons which sometimes blow with incredible violence. I remember during a typhoon, when the storm was at its height, a number of foreigners attempted to rescue two women from a small China boat. Their tiny vessel was as nearly as possible in the position now occupied by the yacht in the centre of the picture, and was kept there by the desperate efforts of the boatwomen, who strove to prevent it from being dashed against the Praya wall, which, having been entirely broken by the force of the sea, presented a front of jagged blocks of granite, interspersed with the wreck of boats that had been shattered to pieces on the stones. The strength of the wind was so great as to reduce the wild raging sea nearly to a level, catching up in its fury the tops of the waves, and hurling them in blinding spray into, and over the houses. We had to cling to the lamp-posts and iron-boat stanchions, and seek shelter against the walls and doorways. Advantage was taken of a lull in the storm to fire off rockets, but these were driven back like feathers against the houses. Two long-boats were dragged to the stone pier. The first was broken and disabled the moment it touched the water; the second met with a like fate, its gallant crew being thrown into the raging sea. Every effort proved abortive, and as darkness set in the boat and the unhappy women were abandoned to their fate. Next morning the whole length of the Praya presented a scene of wreck and devastation. Many of the natives had lost their lives; and many more, all that they possessed in the world, by the destruction of their boats; for these not only form their floating dwellings, but afford the means of gaining a subsistence. Much of the distress was at once relieved by the prompt liberality of the foreign and native community. This ready open-handed liberality is a characteristic of the foreign communities of Hong-Kong and the other ports of China. A kind of Christian charity is rife among them, requiring no efforts of pulpit oratory, no eloquent private appeals, no public dinners to wake it into action. A simple notification that there is a widow or an orphan to be aided, and the sympathy and funds are forthcoming to provide for them. I must not omit to mention the flagstaff shown on the Peak above the city; one of the early institutions of the Colony, and to which a resident signalman and code of signals are attached. It is an object of solicitous attention among the European community, for it proclaims the approach of every foreign vessel as she enters the Port.

Few who have made Hong-Kong for any time their home, have not watched with earnestness the bare post and spars of the signal staff, and experienced a sense of relief, or a quickened pulsation, as they noticed the little flag unfurled, and the flash from the Peak gun, that heralded the arrival of the mail in the harbour.

VI.

BOAT GIRLS.

THESE are the two daughters of a respectable boating family. They have been trained to the use of the oar, and the management of boats, from earliest childhood. Happy for them they are not slaves, purchased by some designing dame, and destined for a worse fate than the life of careful industry common to the labouring poor of Canton.

The hat worn by the elder sister is made of ratan, closely woven, and varnished so as to render it waterproof; it affords protection from the sun as well as the rain, and serves, indeed, all the purposes of an umbrella. It has, too, this advantage, that, while it shelters the body, it gives the wearer the free use of her arms.

Hundreds of the small passenger boats that ply for hire about the wharves of Canton, are managed by young girls, whose pride it is to keep them bright and attractive-looking. Each boat has a small cabin, open in front, having its floor covered with white matting, a broad, raised seat, covered with like material, on which the passenger will find a tobacco pipe, spills, and the apparatus for procuring a light. The walls of the little cabin are adorned with pictures and small mirrors. The girls propel the boat from behind, and are separated from the passenger by a partition of wood, or bulkhead. Viewed from without, the boat has an equally attractive appearance, every board of the deck has been scoured with sand, until it rivals in whiteness the matting within, while a stand fixed on the bamboo roof of the cabin supports a little garden of favourite flowers. The girls, dressed with modest simplicity, deck their glossy black hair with some bright-coloured flower that heightens the effect of their dark eyes, and olive skins.

A CANTON BOATWOMAN AND CHILD.

MANY thousands of the population of Canton pass their lives in their boats,—in them they are born, and from them they are carried to their graves. These floating dwellings afford many advantages to their poor owners, who, had they to live on land, would be crowded into miserable makeshift hovels in the unhealthiest quarters of the city. There they would have to inhale the polluted air of a neglected neighbourhood, as even in the most·fashionable localities of a Chinese city all sanitary regulations are ignored. In a boat the owner finds profitable employment for himself and his family, and in many instances, a clean, comfortable, and attractive looking home, while he can shift his anchorage at pleasure, and move to where the society may be most congenial to his tastes, enjoying a degree of social intercourse by his nightly changes unknown even to the most favoured of those who dwell upon the land. When he visits his friends his house and family go with him. In time of sickness he moors close to his physicians, in some healthy country district, where an invalid can breathe purer air ; or, it may be, hard by a favourite shrine, where he can solicit the aid of its healing spirit, the efficacy of whose powers has been handed down by tradition, and on whom he implicitly relies.

The old woman in the photograph is the grandmother living with her son's family in the boat ; she still works cheerfully at the oar to help the domestic earnings ; and nurses, all the while, one of the grandchildren. Probably this is the eldest son, the pride of the family, and the hope of her old age. The babe is carried in a cloth slung over the shoulders, after the manner of the Chinese race, and he presses his face against the back of his bearer during his hours of sleep. This custom is so common, as to account, to some extent, for the flat faces and broad noses of the boating and labouring classes in China.

MUSICIANS.

THE theory of music was understood by the Chinese at a very early period. It is recorded in their ancient Classics,[1] that 2000 years B. C., they used six tubes to produce the sharp notes, and six for producing the flat ones in the scale. These tubes were originally made out of reeds or bamboo. Subsequently, when they became the standard measures of the notes, they constructed them of some kind of gem.[2] These tubes, which seem to embody the first idea of the organ pipes, became in time the standards of lineal measure, as well as of sound. I have lately seen in China a small organ, said to be ancient, and in some respects resembling the description of the tubes which Dr. Legge has supplied. It has a small mouthpiece, and a series of orifices on the pipes for producing the different notes. The Laos people in the north of Siam construct a simple organ of reeds at the present day.

The Chinese have a number of plaintive and pleasing airs which they sing or perform on their string and wind instruments. They do not, however, appear to understand the principles of harmony, as a band of musicians either play in unison or produce discord; a strife seeming to exist among the respective players as to who will get through the greatest number of notes in the shortest period of time. Bands of music are hired to dispel malignant spirits and other evil influences, and with, I should think, decided success if these spirits are endowed with musical taste, and appreciate the harmony of sound that, in the tragedy of " Macbeth," appears to have afforded Hecate and her dark sisters a fiendish delight.

> " And now about the cauldron sing
> Like elves and furies in a ring,
> Enchanting all that you put in !"

The two illustrations represent the Chinese violin and guitar, with the performers, who are hired on festive occasions.

---

[1] Translation of " Shoo King," Part II. Book I. Dr. Legge.

[2] One would infer from the following note to " Lalla Rookh," that the ancient Chinese possessed, not only poetical but inventive genius of a rare order. " An old commentator of the Chou-King says, the ancients having remarked that a current of water made some of the stones near its banks send forth a sound, they detached some of them, and being charmed with the delightful sound they emitted, constructed *king* or musical instruments of them."—GROSIER.

> " Through the groves, round the islands, as if all the shores
> Like those of Kathay uttered music, and gave
> An answer in song to the kiss of each wave."
> *Lalla Rookh, The Light of the Harem*, p. 301.

VII.

VII.

VII.

VII.

A CANTON JUNK.

THE term junk, applied by Europeans to all Chinese craft, whether trading vessels or ships of war, is probably derived from " jung " the Javanese word for a large boat or vessel. Chinese ships vary in dimensions, model, and appearance, in the different parts of the Empire as much as do the sailing craft of Europe. The vessel under sail on the left of the photograph is a coasting trader of Kwang-tung build, and may be regarded as one of the clipper fleet of Southern China. It looks heavy and unhandy, but it will make good sailing with a fair wind. The hull consists of a double planking or shell of wood, having the seams carefully caulked with oakum and gum damar; the latter article is largely imported from the forests of the Malayan Archipelago, Siam and Cambodia. The hull of the vessel is strengthened and held together by massive hard-wood beams or girders, sweeping in a triple row from stem to stern. The hold is divided into watertight compartments, so that were an injury sustained, and one or more compartments filled with water, the vessel might still have buoyancy left to float ashore or into dock. This junk is a fine type of its class, and has in her model something of the foreign ship, though retaining quite enough of the old Chinese build to soothe the prejudices of the nation. We can still notice the huge unwieldy rudder perforated to break the force of the sea, for the Chinese have not yet got the length of perceiving that a very much smaller rudder, fully immersed, would be quite as serviceable and infinitely less exposed to the risk of disaster. There, too, are the great eyes, and the configuration about the stem resembling the head and features of a fierce sea-monster, and intended to scare away the deep sea-demons, or huge fish, that might at any time impede the voyage. The mat sails, with their ribs of bamboo, still look like the spread wings of a huge bat, or the fiery dragon of the Celestial Mythology. Her rig, however, is not so unmanageable as appearances would imply; with a fair and willing crew the sails can be set with care and speed, while they will fall if the ropes be unfastened, and furl, without an effort, of themselves. The anchor is of hard wood that has a greater specific gravity than water. The ropes and cables are of ratan, bamboo, or palm fibre, and are so strong that they will stand as great, if not a greater strain than anything in use with us. They have the disadvantage, however, of being less flexible and not so easily stowed. These trading junks are usually well-armed, carrying, at least, half-a-dozen smooth-bore guns of foreign make for six or eight-pound shot, a number of matchlocks, and a quantity of ammunition.

These vessels are frequently owned and sailed by a party of small traders, a number of the better class of sailors having a venture in the cargo as well. This complication of petty interests and the absence of a recognized commander, or indeed of anyone scientifically trained in navigation, leads to constant disputes, and to a total disregard of discipline on the part of the crew, for these are men of the lowest social order, the more respectable and industrious of the labouring classes preferring a shore-life to the hardships and risks of the sea.

In a case of emergency, such as a storm, a consultation takes place as to the fittest mode of handling the vessel, and the decision is frequently referred for final settlement to " Machu "[1] the sailor's goddess, who has a shrine set apart for her on board. Each sailor carries about his person a small bag containing the ashes from some favourite altar of this goddess, and holds them as an infallible charm to ward off shipwreck and the diverse perils of the deep.

---

[1] " Social Life of the Chinese," Doolittle, vol. I. p. 262.

It is customary before proceeding on a voyage to offer sacrifice to " Machu." A cock is decapitated, and its blood, together with some of its feathers, are stuck to the bow and foremast, a small cup of wine is at the same time cast over the bow into the sea. This ceremony of decapitating a cock is also used by the Malays, as well as the Chinese, in taking an oath. I have met with instances of this with both races when a person has been accused of uttering a falsehood, his reply being that he was prepared to take his oath over the head of a cock.

Sailing, as I have above observed, is managed, not by the study of the compass, barometer, or by astronomical observations, but by a knowledge of the currents, and headlands, and the prevailing winds of the season. The compass is used, but it is an instrument of primitive construction, having a very small tremulous needle in the centre of a disc of wood, covered with a formidable array of Chinese symbols, astrological and others. It seems strange that the reputed inventors of the mariner's compass should have left to other nations the merit of applying it to its proper scientific use.

These remarks on Chinese vessels, it must be understood, apply only to trading craft, as it will be hereafter shown that the Chinese have made much more progress in constructing vessels of war.

VIII.

FRONT OF KWAN-YIN TEMPLE, HONG-KONG.

THIS is a small temple on the hill-side, to the east of the city of Victoria. It is dedicated to Kwan-yin, the goddess of mercy, and is liberally supported by the Chinese of Hong-kong. Like the majority of Chinese temples, it has been erected in a position naturally picturesque, and is surrounded by fine old trees and shady walks, commanding an extensive view of the harbour. A never-ceasing crowd of beggars infest the broad granite steps by which the temple is approached, and prey upon the charitably-disposed Buddhists, who make visits to the shrine. These beggars trade upon the knowledge that in the Buddhist it is a meritorious act to help the poor and needy. The temple front is a good specimen of the elaborate ornamentation with which these places of worship are adorned. The direct entrance to the sacred interior is barred by a heavy screen of wood, which stands about six feet within the central door. This screen is a very common piece of furniture in Chinese dwellings, as well as in temples. It serves the double purpose of securing additional privacy to the inmates, while it wards off malignant spirits, which are popularly supposed to travel in direct lines, and not by circuitous routes. Within the threshold, on the right, is a dispensing department, where an apothecary makes up the numerous prescriptions of the goddess; on the left, an aged priest disposes of the paper counterfeits for money, which are bought by the worshippers, and burned as offerings at the shrine. Kwan-yin, a female figure draped in flowing robes and wearing a benign expression of countenance, is observed in the centre of the apartment, seated in a dim recess behind the altar, on which are an array of brazen bowls, vases, lighted candles, and smouldering incense sticks. On the floor, there are a number of straw mats, for the use of the kneeling worshippers, on one of which an aged woman is bent, supplicating the goddess in behalf of a sick son. She is muttering some incoherent prayer, and from time to time looks for a favourable omen, not from the clay lips of the painted goddess,—no, poor soul! her tearful eyes are bent down with solicitude upon two plano-convex bits of bamboo, which, tossed in the air, have fallen on the floor, recording by the sides which lie uppermost a good or bad omen. She pleads with the touching fervour of a fond mother : persistently tossing the sticks of fate, she will take no denial. At length, after many turns of disappointment, she secures a good omen, and proceeds to spend her mite in offerings to Kwan-yin.

A MENDICANT PRIEST.

THIS priest is attached to the Kwan-yin Temple ; his duty is to beg for the benefit of the establishment, and to perform unimportant offices for the visitors to the shrine, lighting incense-sticks, and teaching short forms of prayer. I paid him half-a-dollar to stand for his portrait. He was very wroth, declaring the sum quite inadequate, as the picture had bereft him of a portion of his good luck, which he would require to work up again with offerings. He further informed me that a good run of praying visitors would have paid him much better for his time. He was undoubtedly of an avaricious disposition, and well up in his profession of begging. I would judge, however, from his starved miserable appearance that he was a faithful disciple of Buddha, and that a very small portion of his gains was devoted to his dress or sustenance. He is a type of thousands of the miserable, half-starved hangers-on of monastic establishments in China. Equally indispensable are tribes of loathsome beggars infesting the gates of the temples, and herds of hungry, howling dogs, that live, or die rather, on temple garbage and beggars' refuse.

A STREET IN HONG-KONG.

N the street shown in the picture Hong-kong residents will readily recognize the semi-Chinese, semi-European roadway which leads to Wanchi, Wong-nei-chong, or Happy Valley.

It is chiefly occupied by native shopkeepers, who supply the wants of the soldiers and their families, residing in the extensive barracks of the neighbourhood. Among others, there is a Chinaman who has been some years in California, where he learned the art of foreign shoe-making. He imports the leather from America, and has taught a number of workmen, whom he has in his employ, to make boots and shoes, which for general appearance, for durability, and price, will bear comparison with the best work of foreign manufacture. A number of cane-chair makers reside in the street, and drive a thriving trade with Europeans, furnishing a variety of light easy-chairs for the open verandahs of foreign houses.

In passing along the street at any hour, from sunrise to nearly midnight, one has many opportunities of observing the constant industry of the Chinese. They appear to have no set hours of labour, but work day and night until their tasks are done.

OPIUM-SMOKING IN A RESTAURANT.

HE opium pipe has become an indispensable Chinese luxury, in which the poorest find time and money to indulge. Many of the worst class of beggars are confirmed opium-smokers,—men who have been dragged down from positions of comfort or affluence by the vice. Long lost to all sense of honour and self-respect, and sunk so low as to become the begging pests of their former friends and associates, they would give the last rag that covers them to gratify their passion for the drug that has consumed their reputation, their substance, and their flesh ; such men are a prey to morbid fits of melancholy and depression, leading to frequent suicide. The mode of destroying life, most commonly resorted to by such men, Dr. Young, of Hong-kong, tells me, is by taking a dose of opium refuse or ash. This is carefully gathered, and kept by the opium-shop, or restaurant-keeper, so that it may be procured in quantity sufficient to destroy life. It is usually taken in water, after which the unfortunate will stretch himself out, to die like a dog, in a lane or dust-heap. The narcotic taken in this form is always fatal, as it adheres so tenaciously to the coating of the stomach as to prevent its removal.

The drug sold in the low public opium-shops is of inferior quality, being mixed with opium ash in its preparation. These shops or dens have a noxious atmosphere, heavy with the fumes of opium, which, added to the livid and death-like appearance of the smokers stretched upon the benches, recalls the horrors of a nightmare.

IX.

IX.

IX.

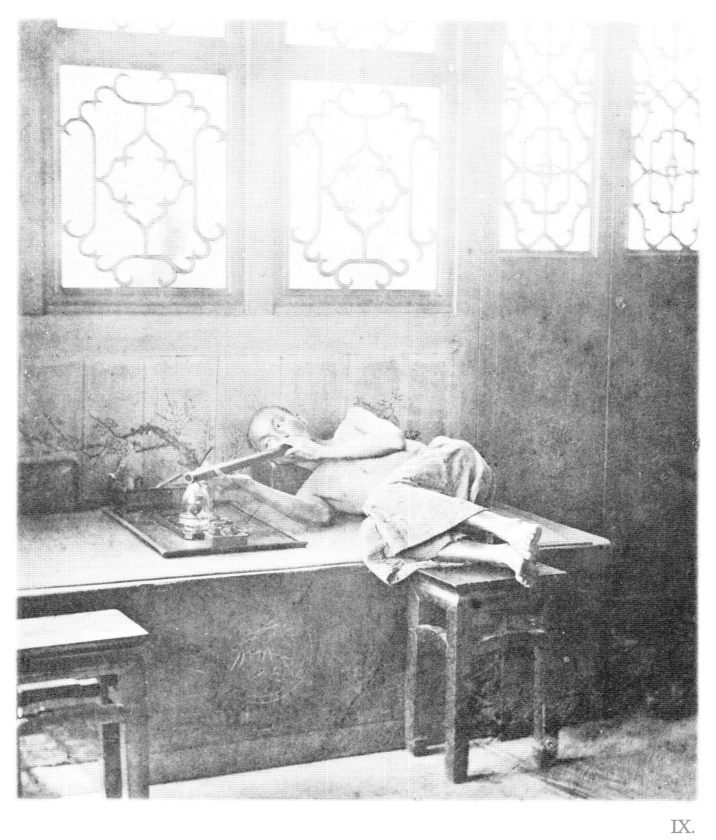

IX.

A WHIFF OF OPIUM AT HOME.

HIS picture shows the method in which opium is smoked by the wealthier classes among the Chinese. The smoker here has leisure and money at his command, so that he is able to indulge freely in the use of the drug. His opium pipe is a formidable-looking instrument, not at all resembling the "hookah" of India, or the light tobacco pipe in use with us. It consists of a metal or bamboo tube, having at one end a wide mouthpiece, and closed at the other. The bowl, of metal, or sometimes porcelain, is usually very ornamental, and has a small aperture on the top into which it receives the drug, which is prepared by the Chinese in the form of an aqueous extract, by boiling the crude opium into the consistency of thick syrup. The smoker when he takes to his pipe must literally lay himself out for his work, and this he does by stretching himself on a bed or couch of polished wood, propping his head with a pillow of the same unyielding material. Near at hand he has a small opium lamp, over which, either he or his attendant, if he can afford one, roasts the tiny pellet of opium on a needle's point before placing it in the bowl of the pipe. All being now ready, the smoker brings his opium-charged bowl once more in contact with the flame and inhales the fume into his lungs, expelling the vapour by his mouth and nostrils when it has been retained for a short time in his body. He must now abandon himself to the influences of the drug, giving up all thought of business or occupation till the effects of the narcotic have passed away.

Opium-smoking is one of the most enslaving vices, which, when it has secured its victim, gradually poisons and destroys the finer feelings of his nature, causing him to neglect his business, dispose of his property, and even sever the sacred ties of kindred by selling his wife and children into slavery so that he may gratify his ruling passion. When once indulged in it is difficult, and sometimes dangerous, to throw off the habit. Were the pipe suddenly withdrawn a painful physical re-action would set in, and death itself has been known to ensue. The smoker may wean himself from the use of opium by taking gradually diminishing inward doses of the drug, which allay the craving for the pipe ; added to this, he must have nutritious food and tonics to restore the tone of his stomach. After a time his desire for the drug will pass off.

The charms of opium must at first be irresistible, as is shown by the multitude of its votaries : but when the habit has been ingrained these exhilarating influences dwindle, and a fearful craving succeeds, which the victim must satisfy at any cost. I know a remarkably clever painter of miniatures, a Hong-Kong Chinaman, who was ruined by opium-smoking at last. Five years ago I recollect him a handsome, fashionably-dressed youth ; his tail a model of perfect plaiting, and his head shaven as smooth as a billiard ball. No silks were more beautiful or richer than his ; while his finger nails, long as vultures' claws, were the envy of his companions and his own secret pride. This good-looking dandy was at that time in full work as a portrait-painter. Some years afterwards I fell in with him again—a shrunken, hollow-eyed, sallow-faced old man. He was still working at his craft, but only on two days a week, the rest of his time being uninterruptedly devoted to the demands of his opium pipe. This instance gives some notion as to the completeness with which the habit may master even young, successful and vigorous men. There are, I am told, many examples of temperate opium-smokers who adhere steadily to a moderate quantity of the narcotic—say a mace a day. I have no reason to doubt the statement ; but, as the practice among men of this class is kept as secret as possible, it is difficult to be certain on the matter.

AFTER DINNER.

HIS is an after-dinner gathering on the verandah of a Chinaman's house. The entire domestic circle smoke tobacco, but their pipes differ from our own. The old woman and her daughter use a pipe which resembles the "hookah," having a small compartment filled with water, for cooling and purifying the smoke. Paterfamilias is fondling and sucking the end of what appears to be a very formidable walking stick ; but it is in reality his favourite pipe, having a cherished history attached to it, and invested with a degree of individuality that appeals to the tenderest feelings of its proprietor. In this we have a trait that reminds us of the regard, bordering sometimes on insanity, which smokers in our own country bestow upon the blackened bowl of an ancient meerschaum. And here let me ask my reader's sympathy for a devoted husband, whom his wife's misguided behaviour drove to the verge of despair. This unfortunate woman, rejoicing, in the unselfishness of a loving nature, to see her husband delighting in a smoke, took advantage of his absence from home to prepare a little surprise; and so his nasty black pipe was, with a world of trouble, carefully scraped, cleaned, and varnished with furniture oil. Alas! this pipe was a relic of bachelor days, a masterpiece of colouring, and mellowed by age, till its fumes were as delicate as the ripened tones of an old violin.

There is then among the Chinese the same after-dinner companionship in smoking which in our own country strengthens the social ties; but with this important difference, that in China the ladies smoke. Among people of higher rank the water-pipe is filled and brought in by a servant, who, waiting till a pause occurs in conversation, adroitly inserts the stem into her mistress's mouth. This custom, to an "outer barbarian," may at first seem strange, and doubly so, perhaps, when he perceives with dismay the swallowed smoke issuing during animated talk from the ladies' nostrils and mouth, belched forth in jets, as if to add force and piquancy to the conversation.

READING FOR HONOURS.

THE rule in China, from the earliest times, has been to confer rank and honours of the highest grade only on men distinguished for rare genius or exceptional literary attainments. By the system of periodical literary examinations established in the chief cities of the Empire, even the poorest student may win his way to a proud position in the government of his country. Who can tell how much the stability of an empire, that for countless generations has remained entire, may owe to such a system as this! Through its agency a healthy influence is diffused among the poorest of the people, binding them more closely to the governing classes, and giving all a common interest in the maintenance of order and peace. Of course, in so large a community many unsuccessful candidates for literary distinction are to be found. Such men as these support themselves by teaching; perhaps they may have passed the lower degrees, and from failing health, incapacity, or old age, can get no further in their career. They, however, meet with universal respect, and are enabled to earn a livelihood by training others for the race. This has been the lot of the venerable scholar in the photograph. He is convinced that there must have been some mistake, or some underhand influences operating in the examinations to which he has been subjected from time to time. He still studies, however, and hopes against hope, that even yet, in his declining years, he will pass with credit to himself and his family, and hold his head with the best. This end attained, he proposes to institute new and improved regulations to suppress corruption in the examinations, and to give men such as he a fair chance of rising to the level, from which nothing but an iniquitous combination has hitherto barred his approach. We rarely find a Chinaman who has not some knowledge of reading, and few parents neglect to devote a portion of their earnings to their son's education, in the hope that his capacities may be so developed as one day to elevate him from obscurity to renown.

THE TOILET.

THE ladies of China are skilled in the use of cosmetics; but their ways are not as our ways. No well regulated Chinese beauty would be guilty of washing her face; it must be polished with a hot damp cloth; when this process is over, the surface is ready to receive its coating of finely prepared white powder. This powder is made up in the solid form of a small disc, neatly fitted into an ornamental paper box, a slight pressure reducing it to a condition fit for use, when it is carefully rubbed into the cheeks, after which the smooth whitened skin is tinted with carmine. The carmine is a Chinese manufacture, and is sold in small books, each page of which is covered with a coating of the dye, and wears a glistening brown-like surface. The lady has only to moisten her finger, and apply it to this pigment, to obtain a beautiful flesh tint, resembling that produced by the coal-dye sold in crystals in this country and designed for a similar use. This she lays artistically over her powdered cheeks. Their mode of removing hair from the face is ingenious. With two fine silken cords arranged upon the fingers so as to yield to the form of the face, and at the same time act as pincers, the lady trims her eyebrows to the proper breadth, and uproots stray hairs from the cheeks, the neck, and even the forehead, if she wishes the latter to appear large and full.

The coiffure presents a variety of styles differing in the different provinces. Hereafter I shall supply some examples of these, which in every instance are most elaborate, and achieved by painstaking manipulation. Many of the patterns of the female headdress are very picturesque and might furnish our own countrywomen with hints. Before the hair is built up into shape it is stiffened with a vegetable gum contained in wooden shavings of a resinous tree, and which exudes therefrom on soaking them in water. The powder, carmine, comb, hairbrush, tooth-brush, tongue scraper, gum, hairpins, and all the other appliances of the feminine toilet, are preserved in a small brass or silver bound dressing-case carrying a mirror within the lid. I must not omit to inform my reader that false hair and even wigs are in common use among Chinese ladies. When the long black tresses have become thin and short, an artificial chignon can be had for a trifle from the barber close by; or, if required for a lady of taste, she will have it made to order by a professional artist of her own sex.

X.

X.

X.

FOUR HEADS, TYPES OF THE LABOURING CLASS.

F the four heads shown in these pictures, the two upper ones are fair types of the aged labourers of China. Darby and Joan have for many years been associated together, and their life has been a uniform scene of hardships and toil. Two generations have now grown up around them, and their sons and grandsons have succeeded them as the bread-winners of the family. The old woman still busies herself in the lighter domestic duties; she is skilful with her needle, and invaluable as a nurse in time of sickness. Her hair has grown thin and white, but she still dresses it with neatness and care.

The old man, who is venerated as the head of the family, gratifies his taste for information by spelling through the cheap literature of the day. This commonly consists of what to us would appear tedious and uninteresting tales, which appeal greatly to the credulity of the reader. The popular books are printed in the more simple and elementary characters of the language, to suit the capacities of the unlettered class. The old man's eyes failed him years ago, and the use of spectacles was reluctantly forced upon him. These spectacles are of native manufacture, having larger and heavier frames than those which our great-grandfathers wore. The lenses, like our own, are double convex or double concave, to suit peculiarities of vision; and being made of the finest rock crystal, they possess advantages only appreciated by us at a comparatively recent date. It seems that the Chinese have not so extended this knowledge as to construct microscopes and telescopes. But this branch of optics is now being taught by foreigners in the Foochow Training School.

The two lower heads are those of a son and daughter belonging to the same class. The male is stripped to the waist, as is his wont during the hours of toil. His plaited queue is at such times coiled up out of the way and fixed with a bamboo bodkin at the back of the head. When work is over he will put on his jacket, and betake himself to the nearest barber's, that the front of his head may be shaved. He is a type of the coolies who used to be kidnapped and sent to South America to labour in plantations or mines. Thousands of these men have emigrated to the United States, and have there left a lasting monument to their industry in the great embankments of the Pacific Railroad.

The female head is that of an unmarried woman, engaged with her family in the management of a cargo boat, used in the loading and unloading of ships. The cloth on her head is worn as a protection from the sun. The hair of unmarried women of this class, combed back and plaited into a queue behind, is then coiled up and fastened with a silver pin. In front it is allowed to fall over the forehead, like a silken fringe. After marriage, it is dressed in the form of the old woman's coiffure.

XI.

XI.

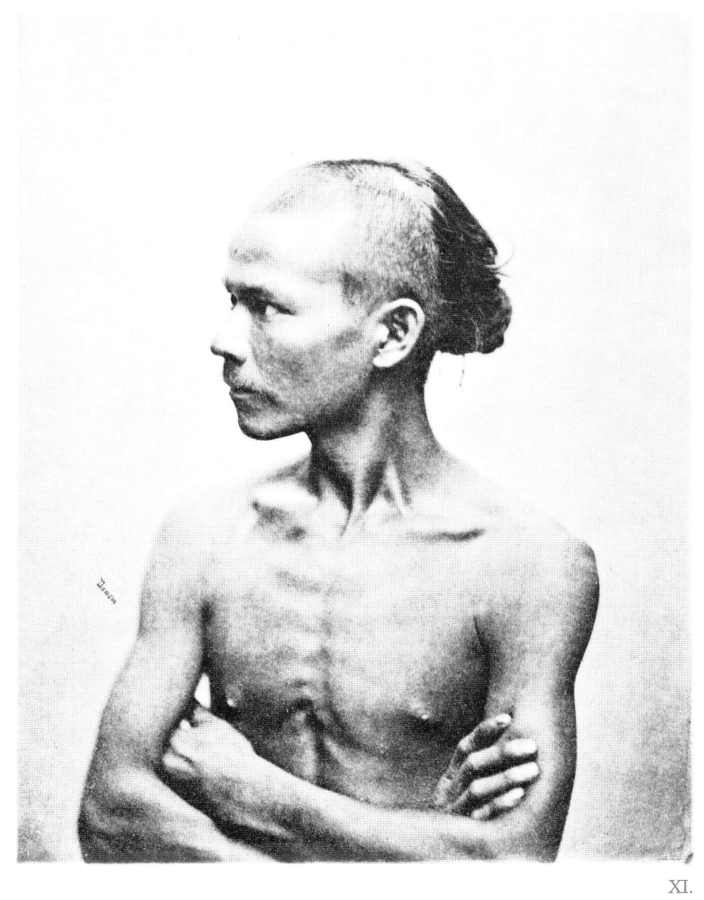

XI.

XI.

HOI-HOW, THE PROPOSED NEW TREATY PORT, ISLAND OF HAINAN.

HAINAN is an island off the southern coast of China, and forms part of the province of Kwang-tung. Hoi-how, the chief port there, was first thrown open to foreign trade during the middle of 1872, and an English consul was thereupon appointed to reside at the post. According to the Chinese annals of the Kwang-tung province, Hainan was first occupied by the Chinese A. D. 654.[1] It was celebrated at an early period for its pearl fisheries, and is the place to which Su-Tang-po, a distinguished statesman and scholar of the eleventh century, was banished. Here, too, as in Formosa, the Chinese authorities have been put to trouble in keeping the independent tribes in check, and in both cases the aborigines have been driven back from the sea-board, to find shelter in the mountain fastnesses of the interior.

Hoi-how is situated on the north-west of the island, and the two forts shown in the photograph protect the approach to it from the river. The distance from Hong-kong is about one-and-a-half or two days' steam. The channel at the mouth of the river is a shallow and dangerous one, owing to numerous sand-bars, which are said frequently to shift. The anchorage for trading vessels is at present four miles from the city, to reach which place one must resort to small passenger-boats, which flock to provision the vessels, or to convey their passengers to Hoi-how.

The town is well-built, and, in common with many other cities of China, is surrounded by a massive wall. Its streets also appear cleaner and better kept than those on the mainland. The country, for about twenty miles inland, is flat, diversified here and there with insignificant hills. Beyond these low hill-ranges a chain of mountains appears, presenting a number of irregular peaks. Mr. Swinhoe has estimated the loftiest of them to be 7,000 feet above the sea-level.[2] "The hills we traversed were very lovely—green, chequered by lines of trees crossing one another, like a park at home in a hilly country."

The plain is well-cultivated with rice, millet, sweet potatoes, ground-nuts, and sugar, all of which are grown with great success, having every advantage of soil and climate to assist them. Rice, however, may be regarded as the chief article of produce. The island being further south, is naturally more tropical than any other part of the Kwang-tung province. The cocoa and areca-palms here grow to great perfection, and the oil of the former supplies an important article of exportation. The fruits, with the addition of the Lichee, are similar in kind and variety to those of Singapore or Malacca. The trade of the island has hitherto been entirely in the hands of native merchants.

From what little we know of the Li, or aborigines of Hainan, they appear to resemble the hill-tribes of Formosa and the "Miau-tzu" of the mountains of the mainland of China; but our information as to their habits and language is too slender to form the basis of any definite conclusions. I had two Hainau Chinamen in my employment for upwards of six years, and from them I have heard many stories of the wild mountain-tribes of their native land; but these were evidently too untrustworthy to be seriously taken into account, if we may judge by the persistence with which they affirmed that the wild mountaineers were closely allied to apes, and carried short, stumpy tails appended to their persons.

---

[1] "A History of the Kwang-tung Province, Bowra," p. 19.   [2] "Shanghai Courier," paper by Mr. Swinhoe.

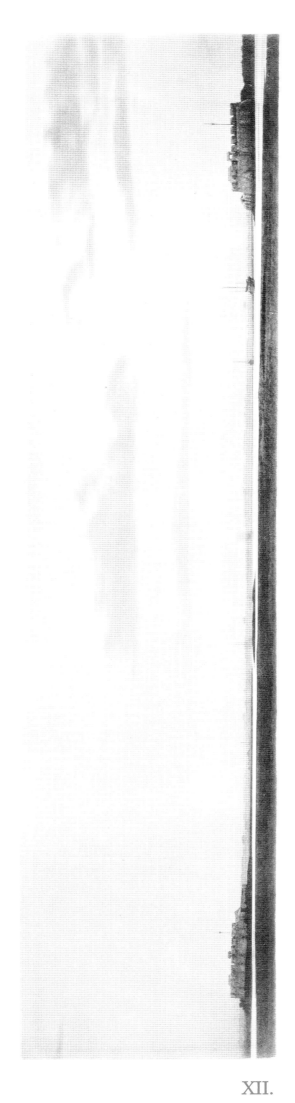

XII.

JUI-LIN, GOVERNOR-GENERAL OF THE TWO KWANG PROVINCES.

THE governor-general (Jui-Lin) of the provinces of Kwang-tung and Kwang-si, familiarly called the viceroy of Canton, from the locality in which his residence is situated, is one of the highest dignitaries in the Chinese empire, and at the same time is, perhaps, of all Chinese officials the most widely known by Europeans. A Manchu by birth, he became at an early age employed in public functions at the capital; and, having gained the favour of the Emperor Tao Kwang, he rose to high employ, reaching at length the dignity of cabinet minister, when about forty-five years of age. After occupying this post for several years, he was degraded from his rank and honours in consequence of the defeat which befell the Chinese forces at the battle of Pa-li Chiao, in October, 1860, on the advance of the British and French forces against Peking. At this engagement Jui-lin officiated as second in command, and narrowly escaped being taken prisoner. Having served subsequently to this period in the operations conducted against the Nien Fei banditti, Jui-lin was re-admitted to favour, and in 1864 was appointed to fill the important office of general commanding the Tartar garrison of Canton. In the following year he took charge of the governor-generalship or viceroyalty of the two provinces on the occurrence of a vacancy, and shortly afterwards was confirmed in this distinguished post, which he has held without intermission until the present day. The importance of his position, and the proximity of the British Colony of Hong-Kong to his seat of government, combine to bring the governor-general into frequent personal relations with European officials, with whom his intercourse has invariably been marked by perfect courtesy, and an obvious desire to cultivate friendly relations. Under his administration the provincial revenue has prospered, a degree of public tranquillity unknown for many years previously has been attained, and ameliorations have been introduced in several departments of the public service, including the organization of a squadron of steam gunboats commanded by European officers, through which piracy, once rampant on the coast, has been almost wholly extinguished. The governor-general was restored in 1869 to the rank of cabinet minister; and in July, 1872, he was promoted to one of the highest posts in the ministry of state. He is at present about sixty-five years of age.[1]

---

[1] The above information was kindly supplied by W. F. Mayers, Esq.

XIII.

TARTAR SOLDIERS.

HE Manchus, commonly called Tartars, conquered China in 1644, but the subjugation at that date was by no means complete, and it was not until the 24th of November 1650, that Canton was taken, or rather delivered into the hands of the besiegers, by the treachery of its governor.[1] The Dutch ambassadors, who were in the city shortly after its capture, thus describe the scene:—

"It was upon the 25th of November, 1650, when the Tartars, upon this advantage, rushed with their whole army into the city, which was soon subdued by them. The besieged not being in a condition to make any resistance.

"The whole Tartar army being got into the city, the place was soon turned to a map of misery; for every one began to tear, break, and carry away whatever he could lay hands on. The cry of women, children, and aged people was so great that it exceeded all noise of such loud distraction, so that, from the 26th of November to the 15th December, there was heard no cry in the streets but, Strike, kill, and destroy the rebellious barbarians. All places were full of woful lamentations, murder, and rapine."

After the overthrow of Canton, the Tartars, following the plan which they had adopted in Peking and other cities of the Empire, established a permanant garrison composed of Tartars and of the Chinese and Mongols that had sided with them. Their encampment remains to this day, occupying about one-fourth of the entire area of the city, and still retaining a few of its original characteristics, although the descendants of the warlike conquerors have lost much of their martial bearing, by adopting the luxuries, and taking up the more objectional characteristics, of the conquered race. " In establishing an encampment there were in equal portions men of the three nations who had accompanied the conqueror from Manchurian Tartary," Manchus, Mongols and Chinese. These were divided under eight banners distinguished by colours, red, blue, yellow, and so forth. In the quarters of the Tartar city occupied by the different banner-men at Peking there is a paper lantern of the banner of the occupant placed on a stand before each door-way.

The banner-men of Canton number 1,800, many of them being extremely poor; for although their nominal pay is good, it never reaches the recipient in full. The government pittance is thus insufficient to support them, and, while during the past two centuries they have been steadily losing their national characteristics, they have scorned to imitate the patient industry of the Chinese, or to adopt their trades and occupations. Hence the great poverty and destitution in many of the mud hovels of the Tartar quarter.

Thoroughly drilled and disciplined, and with a commissariat that would provide effectively for their wants, they would still make good soldiers. Under Jui-lin, the present able governor-general of the two Kwang provinces, a number of Tartar and Chinese soldiers have been instructed in the system of European drill, and in the use of foreign arms.

The reader cannot fail to be struck with the fine manly build and soldierly appearance of the Tartar artillery-men shown in the photograph. These men formed the native guard of Sir D. B. Robertson, our consul at Canton.

---

[1] " A History of the Kwang-tung Province," Bowra, p. 93.

XIV.

A CANTON LADY.

 LADY in China passes her life in strict seclusion. Her little world is her home, her companions the ladies of her own household, or relatives of her own sex. If married, she has a separate suite of apartments for herself, children, and maid servants. If she pays a visit, a sedan chair conveys her from her own door; silken curtains screen her from the public gaze; and thus protected, she is borne to the ladies' quarter in her friend's home, with jealous privacy and concealment. When seated among her friends she partakes of tea and a pipe, and displays in her conversation a far greater knowledge of the outer world than one might at first have expected. In passing through the streets her eyes have been busy between the spaces of her blinds, and she has formed her own impressions of the faces and figures as they went by. However contented she may be, her lot must at least appear monotonous to the ladies of western lands. Her life is hedged round with so many restrictions; she is not even permitted to monopolize the privilege of wearing false hair, for the gentlemen use it extensively, to add to the length and attractiveness of their queues. Neither are they free to dress as they may choose, for there is an Imperial edict which regulates her attire. I question, however, whether this law, which thus hampers the Chinese lady, is a more rigorous despot than fashion, which in our own country sways the gentler sex.

I shall have occasion to notice the Chinese ladies in a future part of the work, and I shall then show the costumes which prevail in different quarters of the Empire.

THE LADY'S MAID.

THIS maid is a slave girl, bought in childhood for a trifling sum from her poor parents, as female children are at a sad discount in many parts of China, where infanticide is still practised. This girl has been reared in the bosom of the family, and trained to wait on the ladies of the household, to attend to the children, and to make herself generally useful. In this picture she is represented on her way to market, the slave enjoying more freedom in going abroad than does her mistress. In her left hand she holds a small lacquered-ware case for cakes and confections, and in her right a huge fan to screen her from the sun. It is wonderful to notice how careful the poorest women in China are of their complexions, how they dread being tanned by the sun, and how universally the fan is employed as a sunshade, as well as for keeping down the temperature of the body; excessive heat and cold being considered two of the leading causes of disease. Even the men delight in a pale skin, and may be seen during summer wearing the fan spread out to shade the face, and fixed to the head by means of the tail.

A BRIDE AND BRIDEGROOM.

Y fair readers will gather from what has gone before that women's life in China is by no means an enviable lot. The monotony of creation with them is enlivened by none of the entertainments which ladies find indispensable in our own quarter of the globe. No balls, no concerts, conversaziones or picnics, no private theatricals, no—not even a lecture—save from a venerated husband's lips, who jealously keeps watch over their actions, and, with careful mistrustfulness, confines them within doors. It has been suggested that the custom of pinching their feet, now regarded as an essential element of female beauty in China, originated in the selfish jealousy of man. For as ladies could not be trusted to go about alone, it was considered necessary to make them cripples, so that they might never appear abroad without attendants to assist them. Be that as it may, unmarried women have very little freedom. To choose future husbands for themselves is a foreign and barbarous custom, and never to be even dreamt of among them : and when the marriage is over they are more slaves than their bondwomen.

Before the wedding takes place, the parties most interested in the contract have little or nothing to do with the arrangements ; all is settled for them by their respective parents or guardians.

There is no period of courtship to distract a lover from his business. It is the Astrologer who has to be consulted. He, for a small consideration, pronounces that the couple are suitable, investigates their horoscopes, and fixes the wedding day. Then the blushing bride (alas, she paints !) is arrayed for the ceremony, and carried from her father's house to the bridal sedan. At the threshold she is held over the flames of a fire, to dispel, as they explained to us, any lurking devilry that might mar her future happiness. The marriage presents are paraded through the street, a band of music accompanies the litter, and away goes the bride to wed some one, no matter whom, selected by the taste of her parents. Dreary and uninteresting from beginning to end is a Chinese marriage ceremony, and in too many cases it must lead to a lifetime of disappointment and tears. In China, as in other parts of the world, ladies prefer, if they can, to get a glimpse of their intended partners. This may be done if circumstances are favourable, but frequently they never see their lord and master, until the day when they are united to him for ever. One can readily fancy that, at such times, the first sight of an ill-favoured face will create a sad feeling of disgust and disappointment.

Filial piety has a strong hold upon the people, and it is esteemed a high virtue to bear in dutiful silence such bitter crosses as these. Let us hope that the time is not distant when these women will be allowed the free use of their natural feet to aid them in the search for husbands. I can fancy I hear some lady saying, " What of their dress ?" The photograph only wants colour to answer the question. The prevailing colour of the dress is red. A bride would as soon do without paint as wed in blue. Blue is the hue of mourning in China—true, it might betoken her mood before the ceremony is over, when her blighted hopes are buried in her bosom. Still, the fair interrogant will say, " Do the creatures never dress in white ? " No, sad to relate ; they would as soon think of breakfasting on the dust of their ancestors as dressing in graveclothes for their wedding ; it is only when bereft of their husbands that they wear white robes.

I will now briefly dispose of the bridegroom by saying, that for the marriage ceremony he is at liberty to wear the robes of a mandarin, thus showing the high esteem in which the relationship imposed by marriage is held by the State, or, it may be, to denote the absolute power which from the day of marriage is vested in the husband as head of the household. He, too, wears red, in the form of a bridal scarf thrown over the shoulder. I must not omit to notice the bride's cap, with its sprays of pearls that veil her face.

It is customary for the poorer members of society to hire their bridal dresses from a costumer, whose business it is to furnish the paraphernalia for wedding and other ceremonies.

XV.

XV.

XV.

XV.

CANTON.

CANTON is the capital of Kwang-tung, the most southerly of the maritime provinces of China, and the province which, above all others, has engrossed the attention of foreign nations. The first authentic notice of Kwang-tung occurs in the native writings of the Chow dynasty, B. C. 1122.[1] The name Kwang-tung was not applied till the fifth century, when the Sung family were in possession of the imperial throne. The Buddhist bonzes, who arrived towards the close of the first century with their religious classics from India, besides being the pioneers of a new faith which has taken deep root in the empire, appear also to have led to the opening of commercial relations between their native country and China. Foreign intercourse with China is supposed to have begun with the reign of the Han emperor Hwan, A. D. 147.[2] It is recorded, however, that a practice of bringing tribute of spices from India commenced some seventy years before this. The intercourse which China has from that time held with outer nations has been subject to periodical interruptions, and its history has been one of endless strife and contention—the Chinese, on the one hand, adhering steadfastly to their policy of exclusiveness, and throwing all kinds of barriers in the way of foreign trade, while nations outside have with equal persistence applied a pressure to which the Chinese have gradually given way, and thus the mutually advantageous treaty-relations have by tardy steps been established.

Canton is situated on the north bank of the " Chu-kiang," or Pearl River, about ninety miles inland, and is accessible at all seasons to vessels of the largest size. Communication between the capital and the other parts of the province is afforded by the three branches which feed the Pearl River, and by a network of canals. A line of fine steamers plies daily between the city and Hong-Kong, and the submarine telegraph at the latter place has thus brought the once distant Kathay into daily correspondence with the Western World. It is a pleasant trip from Hong-Kong up the broad Pearl River. From the deck of the steamer one may view with comfort the ruins of the Bogue forts, and think of the time and feelings of Captain Weddell, who, in 1637, anchored the first English fleet of merchant vessels between what the Chinese, in their ignorance of the outer barbarians, regarded as the jaws of death. From this point the gallant captain, through the jealousy, misrepresentation, and slander of the Portuguese, had to fight his way up to Canton, where he was ultimately supplied with cargoes for his ships, but at such unprofitable rates that the trade was abandoned for more than twenty-five years.

The Portuguese of the Kwang-tung province had done much by their own duplicity to damage the reputation of foreigners, and to confirm the Chinese maxim, that " The barbarians are like beasts, and not to be ruled on the same principle as citizens. Were any one to attempt to control them by the great maxims of reason, it would tend to nothing but confusion. The ancient kings well understood this, and accordingly ruled barbarians by misrule. Therefore, to rule barbarians by misrule is the true and the best way of ruling them."[3] If the Chinese tried our patience by the application of the above maxim, we have returned the compliment with interest by our hard blows, and by a persevering determination which has forced them to throw open their country to the benefits of foreign trade and intercourse—benefits now beginning to show themselves in the gradual development of the natural resources of the country, and in the various branches of native industry which supply our wants. Japan has recently abandoned its long-cherished principle of isolation, courts the friendship of Western nations, adopts their arts, studies their sciences, and even remodels its religion. As the Chinese will find it inconvenient, before the lapse of many years, to have a nation so accomplished so contiguous to their shores, one is almost safe in predicting a like change in the Chinese policy, and that before the end of this century the " Great Middle Kingdom " will have been brought within the pale of that higher civilization whose existence it has so sedulously ignored.

---

[1] Bowra's " Kwang-tung Province," p. 3.   [2] *Ibid.* p. 8.   [3] " The Chinese," Davis, p. 28.

THE OLD FACTORY SITE, CANTON.

IN 1684 a small patch of land on the bank of the river at Canton was granted to the East India Company, with permission to erect a factory there, provided all their traders and trading operations were strictly confined within its circuit. This site, with its present boundary-wall and buildings, surrounded by the miserable makeshift huts of the poorest class of the population, is shown in the photograph annexed. It now forms the American Concession Ground, and its buildings are occupied by Messrs. Russel, and by Messrs. Smith Archer, two of the oldest American houses in China. The appearance of this site in 1751 is well described in Osbeck's "Voyage," where some account may be found of the many dangers and disadvantages to which the merchants of a century ago were constantly exposed. They were restricted from entering the city, and were also held responsible for the payment of the heavy duties on merchandise. Their profits, however, in those days were so enormous as to enable them to retire in affluence after effecting one or two successful shipments. Time has wrought great changes since. While the city of Canton and its people have remained *in statu quo*, a vast foreign trade has sprung up, and multitudes of pale-faced merchants now transact their business with all the facilities which steamboats, telegraphs, and a thoroughly organized system of imperial Customs afford. But rapid fortunes are much more rarely accumulated now than when the factories were flourishing in years gone by. Sha-mien, the British Concession Ground, has taken the place of the "Factory Site;" and its green sward, its rows of trees, its flower-garden and promenade fronting the river, its elegant stone residences, and well-built church, would not disgrace a fashionable suburb in London.

The repellent policy of the Chinese Government subjected foreigners to much humiliation, and ended in a declaration of war in 1839. Canton was ransomed when on the point of being captured by the British forces in 1841, and peace was thereupon re-established by the treaty of Nankin. Notwithstanding the terms of the treaty, the Chinese persisted in closing Canton against foreigners, and their obstinacy culminated in fresh hostilities in 1856. On the 15th of December in that year, the houses on the "Factory Site" were pillaged and burned—on the 29th December the city was captured by the allied forces of England and France, and occupied till 1861.

Canton, although boasting of a great antiquity, has few ancient monuments to show, owing to the perishable nature of the material out of which the houses and public buildings have been constructed. Its wall is about six miles in circuit and thirty feet in height, built of brick on a basement of granite, and backed by an embankment of earth. An inner wall, running east and west, divides the enclosure into the old and new city, the former being approached by four gates, and the latter by twelve. The present population of Canton is estimated at one million.

XVI.

THE BRITISH CONSULAR YAMUN, CANTON.

THE yamuns, or residences of the governor-general and other high officers of the province, are situated in the Tartar quarter of the city. The area covered by each of these yamuns is considerable, for it includes, besides the private dwelling of the mandarin, the courts and offices of his departments in the administration.

We enter the governor-general's yamun by a triple gateway, and pass through a series of paved and highly ornamental courts, overshadowed by the rich foliage of venerable trees, by groves of bamboo, and the huge leaves of the banana. These courts conduct us straight to the official reception hall; beyond this, and approached by a succession of passages adorned with quaint vase-shaped doorways, and a profusion of wood panels carved in the most exquisite designs, are the private gardens and apartments of His Excellency's household. These gardens are embowered in trees, beneath which are pleasant shady walks, winding now round lotus pools, now between strange porcelain walls mantled with a variety of flowering shrubs. Here and there we come upon a little rocky retreat, covered with moss, fern, and lichen; the whole representing the perfection of Chinese landscape gardening; though to a foreigner more attractive for the novelty and beauty of its detail than for the general effect of the whole.

The British Consulate is formed by the rear-half of the Tartar general's yamun. A wall encloses a space of six or seven acres, laid out, for the most part, as a garden or park. In this park are arbours of fine old trees, which afford shade to a herd of deer, so tame that they will feed from their keeper's or the consul's hands.

The consular residence is entered by a round opening in the wall, through which we catch a glimpse, as we approach, of a court adorned with rockeries, of gold fish in vases, and of pots of rare shrubs set in ornamental china stands. The house itself consists of two flats, and is purely Chinese in its construction. The only other buildings of importance in the enclosure are a suite of apartments built in a row, and approached by granite steps, frequently used for the accommodation of visitors. The consular offices and residences of the junior members of the consulate are situated on the British concession of Shamien.

This photograph is taken from the steps of the row of buildings just noticed, showing a portion of the garden; and, in the centre, the ruined gable of a palace, occupied about two centuries ago by the son-in-law of the Manchu conqueror. The pagoda is known to the Chinese as the " Flowery ornate" Pagoda. It is one of the oldest in the south of China, and is said to have been erected during the reign of Wu-Ti, A. D. 537. Its shape is octagonal, it has nine stories, and is 170 feet high. It was scaled in 1859 by some British sailors, but the natives are not allowed to run the risk of an ascent.

XVII.

A CANTONESE PAWN-SHOP.

HE Pawnbroker establishments of the Kwang-tung Province recalled the high square towers I have seen in Scotland, and which, in ancient times, were used as strongholds and places of defence. The square tower in the illustration is a specimen of the pawn-shops throughout the South of China, which lift their heads above the houses, and mark the site of the villages that are scattered over the plains of Kwang-tung. The tower stands close to the side of the old Canton factories, uprearing its bare sides from a plot of ground which is encircled by a lofty wall; while the door by which it is entered is strong as some castle gate. Within, on the ground floor, is the office for the transaction of business, and thence a square wooden scaffolding, standing free of the inner walls, runs right up to the roof. This scaffolding is divided into a series of flats, having ladders as their means of approach. On the ground flat are stowed pledges of the greatest bulk, such as furniture or produce. The smaller and lighter articles occupy the upper flats, while one nearest the roof is exclusively for jewellery or other property of great intrinsic value. Every pledge from floor to ceiling is catalogued, and carries a ticket denoting the number of the article, and the date on which it was deposited. Thus everything can be found and redeemed at a moment's notice. An iron railing and a narrow footpath run round the outside of the roof, and a store of heavy stones is piled up there, to be hurled upon the head of a robber, should he attempt to scale the wall. Valuable property is insecure in this part of the country. This tower is consequently a place of safe repose for the costly jewels and robes of the wealthy classes of the community; besides which, as a licensed pawnbroking establishment, it advances money temporarily to the poor who may have security to lodge. In such establishments three per cent. interest per month is charged on sums under ten taels, save in the last month of the year, when the rate is reduced to two per cent. When over ten taels, the rate is two per cent. per month. Pledges are kept for three years in the better class of pawnshops.

HONAM TEMPLE, CANTON.

ONAM TEMPLE, one of the largest Buddhist establishments in the south of China, stands on the southern bank of the Pearl River at Canton. Passing along the broad granite pavement which conducts from the water-side, and entering the outer porch, beneath the shade of venerable trees, the visitor finds himself within a spacious outer compartment, having gigantic gateways in front and to the rear. Two colossal statues, deities of Indian mythology, and armed and equipped as warriors, present themselves next to his gaze. These are the adopted guardians of Buddha, and in temples even greater than that of Honam these panoptical champions are increased to four. We next ascend by a flight of broad steps to an inner causeway, and the vista shown in the photograph comes thereupon into view. Beyond, in a central court, is the adytum, or inmost shrine, where three images of Buddha glisten with a coating of polished gold. Here the air is laden heavily with the fumes of incense, rising in spiral columns from the altar in front of the gods. A priest tends the burning tapers that from generation to generation have been kept alight; and all round are bowls of bronze, and vases filled with ashes, embers of incense sticks, and the relics of a thousand votive gifts. The candles which burn upon the altar cast a lurid flare over the mystic images and amid the silken hangings of the roof. The constant tinkling of a bell, or the solemn monotonous chant of some aged priest, the surrounding darkness of the dim interior, combined with the worship of a strange god, induce a sense of depression, which is speedily dissipated by a stroll in the wonderful garden beyond. Here the priests delight to tend and rear rare and beautiful plants, dwarf trees, growing marvels in the form of tiny boats and bird-cages, and plants, whose stems are trained into a hundred curious devices. Here, too, is a pen full of fortunate pigs, guaranteed immunity from slaughter, as under the protecting roof of Buddha, the mighty saviour of life.

THE TEMPLE OF THE FIVE HUNDRED GODS.

HIS celebrated shrine, which the Chinese call "Hua-lin-szu," "Magnificent Forest Temple," is situated in the western suburbs of Canton, and was erected by Bodhidharama, a Buddhist missionary from India, who landed in Canton about the year 520 A. D.[1] and who is frequently pictured on Chinese tea-cups ascending the Yangtsze on his bamboo raft. The temple was rebuilt in 1755, under the auspices of the Emperor Kien-lung, and with its courts, halls, and dwellings for the priests, covers a very large space of ground. It is the Lo-Han-T'ang, or Hall of Saints, partly shown in the photograph, that forms the chief attraction of the place.

This Hall contains 500 gilded effigies of saints out of the Buddhist calendar, representing men of different Eastern nationalities. Colonel Yule, in his new edition of "Marco Polo," says that one of these is an image of the Venetian traveller; but careful inquiry proves this statement incorrect, as there is no statue presenting the European type of face, and all the records connected with them are of prior antiquity. The aged figure shown in the next picture is that of

THE ABBOT.

R Chief Priest of this temple. About three years ago, when I paid my first visit to this establishment, in company with a native gentleman from the Canton Customs Office, I was introduced to this Abbot. He received us with great courtesy, conducted us to his private apartments, and there refreshed us with tea-cakes and fruit. The rooms he occupied were enclosed by a high wall, and approached through a granite-paved inner quadrangle, adorned with a variety of rare and beautiful flowers. Conspicuous among the latter was a splendid specimen of the Sacred Lotus, in full bloom, and growing in an ornamental tank, on whose surface floated many other brilliantly green aquatic plants. The old gentleman had spent half his lifetime in this secluded place, and was greatly devoted to his flowers, discoursing on their beauty with an eloquent fondness, and expressing his delight to discover in a foreigner kindred sentiments of admiration. The furniture of the apartments consisted of chairs of skilfully carved black wood, one or two tables, and a shrine of the same material; while a number of well-executed drawings, hung about the white walls, displayed a simple taste and refinement in keeping with the surroundings of their proprietor's secluded life. Two years afterwards I visited the temple again, and executed the photograph here represented. On the second occasion I met with the same kind hospitality at the hands of the Abbot and the priests in his care—a hospitality which, with one exception, I enjoyed in all the Buddhist establishments I visited throughout my travels in China.

---

[1] "A History of the Kwan-tung Province," p. 12, Bowra.

XVIII.

XVIII.

XVIII.

XVIII.

TEA PICKING IN CANTON.

I N former times, before Hankow or the Yangtsze River was thrown open to foreign trade, all the tea from the great Tung-ting Lake district was brought to Canton for exportation. The bulk of the tea shipped now-a-days from Canton is grown in Kwang-tung, of which province that city is the capital.

From the leaf of the Tai-shan plantations, which are the most noted in that neighbourhood, the "Canton District Congou," and the "Long Leaf-Scented Orange Pekoe," are manufactured. These teas are prepared by twisting the leaf in the hand; when so twisted it frequently shows a small white feathery tip at the end of the leaf, known as the "Pekoe tip."

Lo-ting leaf makes "Scented Caper" and Gunpowder teas. These teas are rolled in a bag with the feet until the leaf is twisted into round pellets.

Macao is the port from which the bulk of District Congous are exported, and Canton is famous for its Scented Capers and Scented Orange Pekoe. The green tea trade from Canton is of secondary importance, this tea being chiefly exported to the continental countries of Europe. The cultivation of tea in Kwang-tung, and the consequent export trade from Canton, are on the increase. The business fell off during the war between Germany and France; but this has turned out to be nothing but a temporary check. As the reader will have inferred, the preparation of tea for the foreign markets is carried on extensively at Canton. The Congou and Pekoe teas are brought down from the plantations, rolled by hand, dried in the sun, and then they are in a condition suitable for subsequent firing and preparation for the market. As I shall hereafter have occasion to describe the planting and packing of tea, I will confine my remarks here to a brief notice of the process by which the leaf at Canton is prepared for exportation.

Black teas, after being partially dried in the sun, and slightly fired, are rolled either by the palm of the hand on a flat tray, or by the foot in a hempen bag. They are scorched in iron pans over a slow charcoal fire, and after this spread out on bamboo trays, that the broken stems and refuse leaves may be picked out. It is this operation, which is performed by women or children, that is shown in the photograph. The teas are then separated by passing them through sieves, so as to form different sizes and qualities of tea. The greatest care and economy are observed in carrying all these processes on, the tea-dust being sedulously gathered up and used in forming a very inferior and cheap quality of spurious tea.

XIX.

PHYSIC STREET, CANTON.

HE streets of a Chinese city differ greatly from those of Europe, and are always extremely narrow, except at Nankin and Peking. They are paved crosswise with slabs of stone, usually worn down by the traffic to a hollow in the centre of the path, and this disagreeable substitute for the gutters of European thoroughfares forms the only means by which the rain-water is carried off. The shops in good streets are all nearly uniform in size; a brick party-wall divides each building from its neighbour; all have one apartment, which opens upon the street, and a granite or brick counter for the purpose of displaying their wares. A granite base also supports the upright sign-board, which, as with us in former days, is the indispensable characteristic of every shop in China.

Opposite to the sign-board stands a small altar or shrine dedicated to the God who presides over the tradesman and his craft. This Deity is honoured regularly when the shop is opened, and a small incense stick is lit and kept burning in a bronze cup of ashes placed in front of the shrine.

The shops within are frequently fitted with a counter of polished wood and finely carved shelves, while at the back is an accountant's room, screened off with an openwork wooden partition, so carved as to resemble a climbing plant.

In some conspicuous place stand the brazen scales and weights, ever brightly polished, and adorned with red cloth, which is wound in strips around the beam. These scales are used for weighing the silver currency of the place, for chopped money is but too common among the Chinese. When goods are sold by weight, the purchaser generally brings his own balance, so as to secure his correct portion of the article which he has come to buy.

Physic Street, or, more correctly, Tsiang-Lan-Kiai (our Market Street), as the Chinese term it,—is one of the finest streets in Canton, and, with its varied array of brightly coloured sign-boards, presents an appearance no less interesting than picturesque.

But traversing it is by no means pleasant in wet weather, as the sloping roofs of the shops approach so near to each other that they rain a perpetual shower-bath on every passer by. The narrowness of the streets is intended to exclude the burning sun, and this object is assisted by covering the open space between the roofs with bamboo basket-work, sufficiently open in its construction to admit light and air, and yet an effective shelter from the heat. To each trade its special locality or street has been assigned, and each shop is a perfect counterpart of its neighbour. Here we find none of the display, none of those desperate efforts to secure the lion's share of custom, which competition has fostered in European towns; and nothing fills a foreigner with more surprise than the drowsy indifference among the shopkeepers of China with regard to the disposal of their wares. When a customer enters a shop the proprietor, a grey-headed man perhaps, but conveying by his well-dressed person a profound appearance of old-established honest trading, will slowly and calmly set down his pipe on the polished counter, or push aside his cup of tea, and then inquire politely the nature of his customer's demands. Should he have the article in stock, he will sell it at the price fixed by the members of the guild to which he belongs, or a higher one if he can obtain it; but, should he be discovered underselling his neighbour, he would be subjected to a heavy penalty.

The streets of the city of Canton are irregularly built and tortuous in their course; those of the poorer sort are much narrower than the one shown in the photograph; they are badly kept, filthy, and even more offensive than the most crowded alley in London, the right of way being contested between human beings, domestic pigs, and undomesticated mongrel curs.   The shops and houses are built of light inflammable material, and a row of earthen pots of water disposed along the roof of each tenement is the sole precaution adopted to prevent the ravages of fire.

I am indebted to Mr. W. F. Mayers, the well-known Chinese scholar, for the translation of the sign-boards of Physic Street, and for the interesting note which follows on Schroffing dollars.

The signboards may be taken as fair examples of the street literature of China, showing the national tendency of the shopkeepers to introduce their commonest wares by some high-flown classical phrase, having, so far as I can see, no reference whatever to the contents of the shop.   Tien Yih (Celestial Advantage), for example, offers a thoroughly terrestrial advantage to customers in the shape of covers and cushions ; and why, one might be tempted to ask, should swallows' nests be a "Sign of the Eternal ?"

These phrases are, however, simply intended as the signs, or names by which each shop is known, as with us in olden times, we used to have the "Golden Fleece," "The Anchor," and the quaint signs of our wayside inns.

Kien Ki Hao.—The sign of the symbol Kién (Heaven).   Hwei-chow ink, pencils, and writing requisites.

Chang Tsi Tang (Chang of the family branch designated Tsi).   Wax-cased pills of select manufacture.

Tien Yih (Celestial advantage).   Table-covers, chair-covers, cushions for chairs, and divans for sale.

Tien Yih Shên (Celestial advantage combined with attention).   Shop for the sale of cushions and rattan mats.

Yung Ki (sign of the Eternal) Swallows' Nests.

Money-schroffing taught here.[1]

K'ing Wēn T'ang.—The Hall of delight in Scholarship.   Seals artistically engraved.

---

[1] The art of "schroffing," or of detecting spurious coin, and of ascertaining the difference between dollars of various issues, is very extensively practised in China, and is studied as a profession by hundreds of young men, who find employment in banks and merchants' offices.   The establishments where " schroffing " is taught, are well-known to be in direct communication with the counterfeiters of Mexican dollars and other coin, and it has often been remarked that the existence of schroffs and of false money are mutually indispensable to each other.   If the amount of counterfeit coin in circulation were less, the necessity for a multitude of schroffs would not be so severely felt as at present ; and if the establishments where schroffage is taught did not exist, the counterfeiters would lose their principal means of passing false money into circulation.

XX.

ROLLING SCENTED CAPER AND GUNPOWDER TEAS.

THE manipulation required to produce Gunpowder Tea is one of the most curious and interesting of all the processes to which the leaf is submitted. The visitor, upon entering the Gunpowder department of a Tea House, is surprised to find a number of able-bodied coolies, each dressed in a short pair of cotton drawers, tucked up so as to give free action to the naked limbs. It is puzzling, at first, to conjecture what these men are about. Can they be at work, or is it only play? They rest their arms on a cross beam, or against the wall, and with their feet busily roll and toss balls, of perhaps a foot in diameter, up and down the floor of the room. One soon perceives, however, that it is work they are after, and hard work too. The balls beneath their feet consist of canvas bags, packed full of tea leaves, which, by the constant rolling motion, assume the pellet shape. As the leaves become more compact, the bag loosens, and requires to be twisted up tightly at the neck, and again rolled; the twisting and rolling being repeated until the leaf has become perfectly globose. It is afterwards divided through sieves into different sizes or qualities. The scent or bouquet of the tea is imparted after the final drying and scorching, and before the leaves have become quite cool, by intermixing them with the chloranthus, olea, aglaia, and other flowers. These flowers are left in the baskets of tea until it is ready for packing, and are then removed by passing the tea through a sieve.

WEIGHING TEA FOR EXPORTATION.

WHEN the market is about to open, the new teas are sorted out into qualities, or "chops," as they are usually termed. Samples of these assorted teas are then submitted to the foreign merchants, who carefully test the colour, size, make, taste and smell of the leaves, and their general appearance, wet and dry. When the professional tea-taster has settled all these points, a bargain is struck for so many thousand chests of the various descriptions of tea, and a day is appointed for examining and weighing the whole. The process of weighing is as follows:—The lead-lined chests (with which we are all familiar), soldered up and ready for exportation, are piled in symmetrical blocks in the weighing-room of the Chinese tea-house. Narrow passages are left between the rows to admit the foreign inspector, and he places his mark upon a score or more of chests, and directs them to be removed, opened and examined on the spot. This done, they are conveyed to the scales, and it is now that the caution of the inspector is called most prominently into play, for experience has taught the practised Chinese weigher how to poise his apparatus by placing his hands lightly upon the ropes of the balance, so that, by a slight effort on his part, the scale may be made to turn either way and confer an appearance of favour on a purchaser, whom in reality he is cheating out of his goods. Fair dealing, however, is as much a characteristic among Chinese merchants of repute as among the mercantile classes of our own community, and the tea chests selected, as described, from the bulk of the cargo, generally show that the transaction has been fulfilled with scrupulous honesty and exactitude.

A TEA HOUSE, CANTON.

THE native tea-firing establishments of Canton adjoin the river, or the banks of a creek, and a granite or wooden wharf is one of their most indispensable accessories.

A number of men may be seen during the tea season in the front of the house, employed, as shown in the photograph, in picking, sampling, and sorting the tea, or in preparing the chests for its reception. Just within the entrance are one or two offices, where the partners, treasurer, and book-keeper pursue their various avocations; while, out of doors, are a number of forms and chairs, and a small table bespread with hot tea and cups, set in readiness for the accommodation of visitors. Beyond is a large apartment for storing the tea; it is here also it is weighed and prepared for exportation. After this we enter an open court, and pass into a firing, picking, sorting, and packing department. Above this chamber there is usually a loft where women and children are engaged in removing the stalks and refuse from the bamboo trays on which the tea is spread out. These trays are ranged in rows on long narrow tables, round which a closely packed throng of pickers and sorters ply unceasingly their busy occupation. This room presents the most animated scene in the house. Many of the women are pretty or attractive-looking, and move their small well-formed hands with a marvellous celerity, pouncing upon and tossing aside the smallest fragments of foreign matter which may chance to have become admixed with the tea, and which none but a thoroughly trained eye could ever have discovered at all. It is impossible to visit an establishment of this kind and not be impressed with the orderly habits and business-like atmosphere of the place, where a thoroughly organized system of divided labour has produced from the leaf of a single shrub so many varieties of one of the most delicate and salutary of the luxuries we possess.

A TEA-TASTING ROOM, CANTON.

THIS photograph represents two Chinese tea merchants in a foreign taster's room, awaiting an offer for their samples. Every foreign house in Canton that does any trade in tea has a room specially fitted up for the accommodation of the taster. The windows of the room have a northern aspect, and are screened off, so as to admit only a steady sky-light, which falls directly on the tea-board beneath. Upon this board the samples are spread in square wooden trays, and it is under the uniform light above described that the minute inspection of colour, make, and external appearance of the leaves takes place. On the shelves around the room stand rows of tin boxes, identical in size and shape, containing registered samples of the teas of former years. These are used for reference. Even the cups, uniform in pattern, and regularly ranged in rows along the numerous tables required, have been manufactured especially for the business of tasting tea. The samples are placed in these cups, and hot water of a given temperature is then poured upon them. The time the tea rests in the cups is measured by a sand-glass, and when this is accomplished all is ready for the tasting. All these tests are made by assistants who have gone through a special course of training, which fits them for the mysteries of their art. The knowledge which these experts thus acquire is of great importance to the merchants, as the profitable outcome of the crops selected for the home market depends, to a great extent, on the judgment and ability of the taster.

XXI.

XXI.

XXI.

CANTONESE GENTLEMEN.

HE elder of the two gentlemen represented by the portraits before us is one who, in early life, devoted himself assiduously to the study of literature, and who, having obtained one or two degrees at the government civil examinations, and displayed a competent acquaintance with the classics, laws, and history of China, got his name enrolled as an unattached member of the Chinese civil service. In process of time he became a salaried official, and a mandarin of the sixth grade. When dressed in official costume, his rank is denoted by the style of his robes, and by the ornaments which adorn them, as well as by the colour and material of the button which surmounts his hat. The pay which he receives from government is small—probably not exceeding twenty pounds a year. This sum he is, however, at liberty to augment, by a system of bribery and extortion, to £1,000, or as much more as can be had in the ordinary course of his duties. Mr. Meadows [1] gives an instance of a mandarin whose annual legal income amounted to £22, and who complained bitterly that his supplemented revenue did not exceed £2,333.

The other portrait is that of a compradore, or treasurer in a foreign mercantile house—a man who, by his legitimate savings and private trading speculations, has accumulated a large fortune. It is the common practice of foreign merchants to employ a Chinaman of known repute and ability to act as treasurer to the firm. All the financial transactions of the house pass through this man's hands—he must therefore be one who merits the full confidence and support of his employers. He is a leading man among the native merchants, a member of their best clubs and guilds, and one whose intimate knowledge of foreign business diffuses a wide-spread influence among the wealthy traders who dwell at the Treaty Ports. This influence is unmistakeably one of the chief causes which induce Chinamen of means to become shareholders in foreign steam navigation companies, and in other commercial enterprises. The position of a Chinese compradore in a foreign house affords a striking example of the clannishness, or strong feeling of kinship, which binds the race together, and operates advantageously on the community at large. Thus the compradore is the head of his clan—all the native servants, and they are numerous in large foreign establishments, are engaged by him—and he it is who is held responsible for their honesty and good behaviour. The whole of the servants—from the coolie who carries the water, to the butler of the household—are members of the compradore's clan; and so thoroughly united are they, that they are careful to avoid disgracing their chief by any breach of good faith.

SCHROFFING DOLLARS.

CHROFFING, or testing and examining dollars, is an operation conducted by the compradore's staff in receiving payment for cargoes, to ascertain that no counterfeit coin has been introduced. These tests are managed with dexterity and speed. In transferring the dollars from one sack to another, two are taken up at a time, poised upon the tips of the fingers, struck, and sounded, the tone of base metal being readily detected. The milling of the edge is also examined, as the Chinese show great cleverness in sawing the dollar asunder, scraping out and re-uniting the two halves, which they fill up with a hard solder made of a cheap metal, that when rung emits a clear silver tone. So deftly is the re-uniting done, that none but an expert can detect the junction of the two halves. When the dollars have all been schroffed, payment is made by weight.

---

[1] Meadows' "Notes on China," p. 100.

REELING SILK.

HE superstitious dread with which the people regarded my photographic apparatus rendered it impossible for me to obtain more than this single picture in the silk-producing districts, although I had made a special journey thither, with the intention of securing a full series to illustrate the various operations connected with this branch of industry. The mulberry grows to perfection in the Kwang-tung province, and is used extensively in the rearing of the silkworm. This business gives profitable occupation to thousands of the families of small farmers, who set aside a portion of their gardens for the culture of the mulberry shrub. On the wives and daughters of the household falls the business of superintending the various delicate operations connected with the production of the silk—their duty it is to collect the eggs, to watch with care the process of hatching, which takes place in April, to nourish with the tender mulberry-leaves the tiny worm as he accomplishes his marvellous labours, and then, when he has finished his silken fabric, to arrest his career of industry, and wind off the cocoons for exportation to the looms of Europe. We owe much to China; and perhaps a knowledge of the rearing of the silkworm, and the introduction of silk are two of the greatest boons she has conferred upon Western nations. It was one of my most interesting experiences in the country to observe how modest were the aspects of this wide-spread industry, and how humble, yet sedulous, were the poor labourers whose lowly toil results at last in robes so magnificent and so dearly prized. In the village where the photograph was taken, all the women, as well as the children of sufficient age, were engaged in reeling silk. The machines are of a very primitive make, the most advanced and perfect being the one here shown. The labourers will not permit the introduction of anything more complex; and their guilds or trades' unions are so well organized that they can hold their own against their employers. This opposition offered by labourers in China to the introduction of new appliances that would tend to expedite labour is akin to what prevails in India. When extensive cuttings had to be made for railroads, the government furnished wheelbarrows to the coolies as a substitute for their small native baskets. The men used the wheelbarrows by placing a basketload in each, and marching off with the barrow mounted on the head. The Chinese workman is a very independent character, who, if he conceives he is wronged by his employer, has effectual means of redress. An English merchant in Hong-Kong gave me a striking example of the combined power of Chinese operatives. My friend had been in the habit of furnishing yellow metal in sheets of a certain thickness, to a coppersmith in Fatshan, the Birmingham of southern China. Some metal a shade thinner was offered—the smith said it would suit admirably, and would save labour. The thin metal, however, was submitted to the men, who at once decided to strike work were it introduced, as it would rob them of the time and labour consumed in beating metal of the old kind and shape, and thus give the master an undue advantage. The metal was accordingly rejected.

XXII.

XXII.

XXII.

XXII.

MACAO.

ACAO, in ancient times a small island off the mainland of Hiang-shan in the Kwang-tung Province, has since been united to the coast by a sand-bar. This occurrence so disgusted the Chinese, that in 1573, shortly after the troubles which the settlement of a few Portuguese at Macao involved, they built a barrier across the bar, with a view to exclude the foreigners from intruding into the interior of the country. The Chinese account of the early Macao Portuguese, and of the manner in which the colony was established, differs materially from that supplied by the Portuguese writers. It appears that, about the beginning of the sixteenth century, the Portuguese had attempted to form trading factories at Ningpo, and near Swatow. These they were compelled to abandon. In 1552 they are said to have obtained permission from the Chinese Government to erect mat-sheds for storing goods at Macao. This, then, seems to have been the germ from which the city has grown to its present proportions.[1] "Fortifications and a church were among the first building works undertaken. Ground-rent was not demanded by the Chinese Government until long after the settlement was formed—not, in fact, until 1582." "About 1580 Macao was erected into an episcopal see by Gregory III., and thirteen bishops have been consecrated in succession to this port." Macao was in its most flourishing condition shortly before the conclusion of the war with Great Britain and the establishment of our colony at Hong-Kong.

It was just prior to these events that the best houses were erected, and the place gradually assumed its present picturesque appearance. The principal residences front the bay, round which runs a broad carriage-drive, known as the Praya Grande, shown in the illustration. This picture was taken from the hill above Bishop's Bay, at the southern extremity of the Praya. The inner harbour is on the north-west side of the peninsula, and here the oldest part of the town is to be found. A number of narrow dingy lanes lead from the Praya to the main streets in the upper part of the town; and here the houses wear an interesting, antique appearance, greatly marred, however, by a variety of bright colours with which the owners daub their dwellings, alike regardless of symmetry and harmony of combination. To a European the effect is as distasteful as a glowing patch of carmine on the shrunken cheeks of a faded beauty. There is now hardly a sign of trade in these once busy streets—or, indeed, of active life in any form—save at noon when tawny worshippers hasten in crowds to the cathedral, or during the evening promenade on the Praya, when the band is playing in the gardens. Influences—local, social, climatic—and fusion of races have dealt unkindly with these descendants of the early Portuguese. They suffer greatly by comparison with the more recent arrivals from the parent land, being smaller in stature, and darker in complexion, than either the Portuguese of Europe or the native Chinese. There are, of course, rare and notable exceptions, but one seldom meets with a moderately well-formed and attractive countenance. This, it must be understood, applies to the lower orders of the population, and to those only among them who are of mixed blood.

The same result may be noticed among the Portuguese in Malacca, where it would often be hard to perceive the faintest trace of Western origin, but for the presence of some article of European apparel—a beaver hat for example—passed down in succession from father to son, and still held an indispensable element in a costume

---

[1] "Treaty Ports of China and Japan," p. 204.

displaying a ludicrous compromise between native and foreign attire. Macao forms a pleasant resort during summer for the residents of Hong-Kong. A steamer plies daily between the two ports, and occupies about four hours in accomplishing the run. A good hotel stands on the Praya Grande, and from its verandah one may enjoy the sea-breeze and the view of the bay, where fleets of fishing-boats lie at anchor, or sail to and fro among the islands. Three times a week travellers may take steamer to Canton, and make the tour of that ancient and most interesting city. There are many picturesque walks in and around Macao, and retired sandy bays invite the wanderer to taste the luxury of a sea-bath. In the garden, now included in the grounds of a private residence, stands the grotto of Camöens, who is said to have resided there when he composed the greater part of Lusiadas, or the Epic of Commerce, as it has been termed. The career of Camöens, both before and after his residence in Macao, was one of strange adventure. " As a soldier, he fought in the empire of Morocco, at the foot of Mount Atlas, in the Red Sea, and in the Persian Gulf. Twice he doubled the Cape, and was led by a deep love of nature to spend sixteen years in watching the phenomena of the ocean in the Indian and China seas. Camöens was banished to Macao in 1556, on account of certain satires which he wrote against the Government "[1]—a summary treatment adopted for the suppression of poets and men of genius in other countries as well as Portugal, and not wholly unknown even in modern times. Macao since 1848 has earned an unenviable notoriety for its traffic in coolies. These unfortunate men were shipped to Cuba, Peru, and other ports on the South American Coast, and were, many of them, kidnapped in the province of Kwang-tung or the islands round about. Shut up first in Macao barracoons, they were thence packed off in crowded ships—inhuman treatment frequently leading to mutiny and massacre, or disease and death, perhaps, bringing to these poor bondsmen a last but grateful relief. That this is no exaggeration the following extract may show :—" The ship 'Dea del Mare' left Macao in October, 1865, bound to Callao. On touching at Tahiti she had only 162 emigrants alive out of 550."

The coolie trade of Macao is now under a strict surveillance, and is mainly indebted to the enlightened administration of the present governor for this urgently needed reformation.

---

[1] " A History of the Kwang-tung Province," Bowra, p. 84.

XXIII.

A MOUNTAIN PASS IN THE ISLAND OF FORMOSA.

THE island of Formosa stretches between 26° and 23° north latitude. It is about 250 miles long, and has an average breadth of 60 miles. A high mountain range bisects the island from north to south, and its peaks may be descried from the mainland when the weather is clear. The place is claimed by the Chinese, and is included as a dependency in the government of Fukien, off which province it lies. The central range of mountains, together with the lower ranges to the west, the spurs thrown off to the east, and a great portion of the eastern coast, are still inhabited by aboriginal and independent tribes. These, in configuration, colour, and language, resemble Malays of a superior type. Akin to them are the Pe-po-hoans, who dwell on the low hill lands and plateaux to the west of the central mountain chain. These Pe-po-hoan tribes are partially civilized, supporting themselves by agriculture, and being to some extent subject to the Chinese yoke. Outside of these districts, and occupying the fertile plains on the west, Chinese planters from the Fukien province are to be found : and intermingled with them are the Hak-kas, a hardy, industrious, and adventurous race, who emigrated from the north of the empire. The Hak-ka Chinese hold lands nearest to the savage hunting-grounds. They also make alliances with the mountain tribes, and carry on trade of barter, exchanging Chinese wares for camphor-wood, horns, hides, ratan, etc.

The present population of Formosa is probably 3,000,000. The island is growing rapidly in commercial importance in consequence of the remarkable fertility of its soil. The cultivation of tea has recently been introduced in the northern districts of the island, and is now carried on there with considerable success ; camphor, coal, and timber of many valuable kinds are plentiful, and enormous quantities of sugar and rice are exported to the mainland from the south. The great mineral wealth of the island is rather a matter of conjecture, as the central mountain ranges remain practically unexplored.

The Chinese claim to have found Formosa towards the beginning of the fifteenth century.[1] Probably the enterprising discoverer descried it from the mainland about that time. The island, however, did not become of much note until it was handed over, in 1614, to the Dutch, and they thereupon built fort Zelandia on an islet off the present capital Taiwanfu. This fort was intended to protect an inner harbour, but this has now totally disappeared, and an arid plain, uniting the islet to the mainland, is all that at present remains of the harbour. In 1661, Koksinga, that celebrated Chinese rover or sea-king, having brought his fleet past the fort into the inner harbour, succeeded ultimately in dislodging the Dutch, took possession of the island, and proclaimed himself king of Taiwan (Formosa). The island was afterwards surrendered to the imperial government by Koksinga's successor, and it is only within the past few years, since the opening of the treaty ports, that its real wealth and resources have become known.

The view of the mountain-pass, taken near La-ko-li, on one of the lower spurs of the central mountains, is intended to convey an idea of the grandeur of the scenery which is to be found in the interior of this "Isla Formosa."

See " Treaty Ports of China and Japan."

XXIV.

THE MAKING OF THIS EDITION.

IN many ways, the late George Eastman is to thank for this edition of John Thomson's seminal photo-history of China. How fitting that the founder of Kodak would be the connection to a groundbreaking work of photography.

With the exception of the new foreword for this edition, the pages you are looking at are facsimiles of the original contained in Volume I of the *Illustrations of China and Its People* housed in the collections of the George Eastman House museum in Rochester, New York. (We've added the gold color to the ornamented text, plus page numbers and plate numbers.)

The staff at Eastman House graciously opened their archives of rare books to us, and as soon as we set eyes on this book of photographs by a one-time optician's apprentice, we felt the stirrings of a new Levenger Press edition. Here was a book with not only stunning images but meticulously crafted narrative portraits of a period and place otherwise lost to history.

Today most facsimiles are created using scanners, but the Eastman House copy of Thomson's book required an even more finely-honed method. For one thing, the book's large format overpowers many traditional scanners. More important, pages as fragile as these need to be handled with extra care. The scanning process can put pressure on a binding because an open book must be laid flat on the top of the machine.

In addition, the pictures in the Eastman House volume are collotypes, a photographic process that was revolutionary in its day and that rendered finely detailed images. So to capture this level of detail for the facsimile—and to protect the original volume—every original was digitally photographed eight times, the camera homing in on a different section of the image each time. These eight images were then "stitched" together electronically into one image for each page.

The greater the number of pixels in an image, the sharper the resolution. Current consumer-model digital cameras average around six to eight megapixels. By contrast, each of these high-resolution images is the equivalent of a photograph taken with a 135-megapixel camera. The result is a near-perfect replica of the original.

The high resolution also made it possible to enlarge, for the first time in print, those images that had been featured in quartet fashion in the original. Instead of one page containing four small images, we give you four pages that each contain one image, the better to reveal the remarkable detail. You will find these in Plates IV, VII,

IX, X, XI, XV, XVIII, XXI and XXII. (In Plate XI, the first two photographs are the "upper ones" the author describes on page 69; the last two photographs are the "lower heads.")

John Thomson was the Marco Polo of his day. The Eastman House describes him as "a pioneering visual anthropologist." Today his photographic equipment would be cumbersome in the extreme, while his "novel experiment" of creating a photographic travelogue is commonplace. But the picture of China he gives us—not only through his photographs but also through his commentary—is an elegant reminder that histories, unless recorded, will mostly be forgotten.

In our century it is relatively easy for most of us to travel to China. Even so, we cannot witness the China that Thomson did. As Michael Meyer says, we can only glimpse it. All the more reason, we felt, to preserve this history and its experience for another century.

ABOUT MICHAEL MEYER.

I N Michael Meyer's first book, *The Last Days of Old Beijing: Life in the Vanishing Backstreets of a City Transformed* (Walker & Company, 2008), he bears witness to a rapidly changing country from his vantage point in one of Beijing's ancient neighborhoods, along its disappearing side streets, *or hutong*. A longtime teacher who first went to China in 1995 as a Peace Corps volunteer, Mr. Meyer has trained China's UNESCO World Heritage Site managers in preservation methods on behalf of the National Geographic Society's Center for Sustainable Destinations. In his second book on China (Walker & Company, forthcoming), he moves from city to country and looks at daily life on a farm in rural China.

We invite your comments about this book.

Please visit the Books section of Levenger.com and click on the book's title to write your review.

UNCOMMON BOOKS
FOR SERIOUS READERS.

A Fortnight in the Wilderness
Alexis de Tocqueville

Gnomologia—1732
The proverbs that inspired
Benjamin Franklin

The Grimani Breviary
Foreword by Ross King

The Happy Warrior
The life story of Sir Winston
Churchill as told through the
Eagle comic of the 1950s

**Jerusalem: The Saga of
the Holy City**
Benjamin Mazar et al.

**John F. Kennedy: The Making of
His Inaugural Address**
Commentary by Roger G. Kennedy

**The Little Guide to Your
Well-Read Life**
Steve Leveen

The Making of The Finest Hour
Speech by Winston S. Churchill
Introduction by
Richard M. Langworth

Notes on Our Times
E. B. White

On a Life Well Spent
Cicero
Preface by Benjamin Franklin

On Becoming Abraham Lincoln
John T. Morse Jr., 1893

On Contentedness of Mind
Plutarch
Introduced by Ralph Waldo Emerson

Painting as a Pastime
Winston S. Churchill

Samuel Johnson's Dictionary
Edited by Jack Lynch

The Sarajevo Haggadah
Authorized facsimile of the
14th-century original

The Silverado Squatters
Robert Louis Stevenson

**Sir Winston Churchill's Life
Through His Paintings**
David Coombs
with Minnie Churchill
Foreword by Mary Soames

Levenger Press is the publishing arm of

LEVENGER®

Levengerpress.com   800.544.0880

**To write your review of this book or any Levenger Press title,
please visit Levenger.com and type the book title into the Search box.**

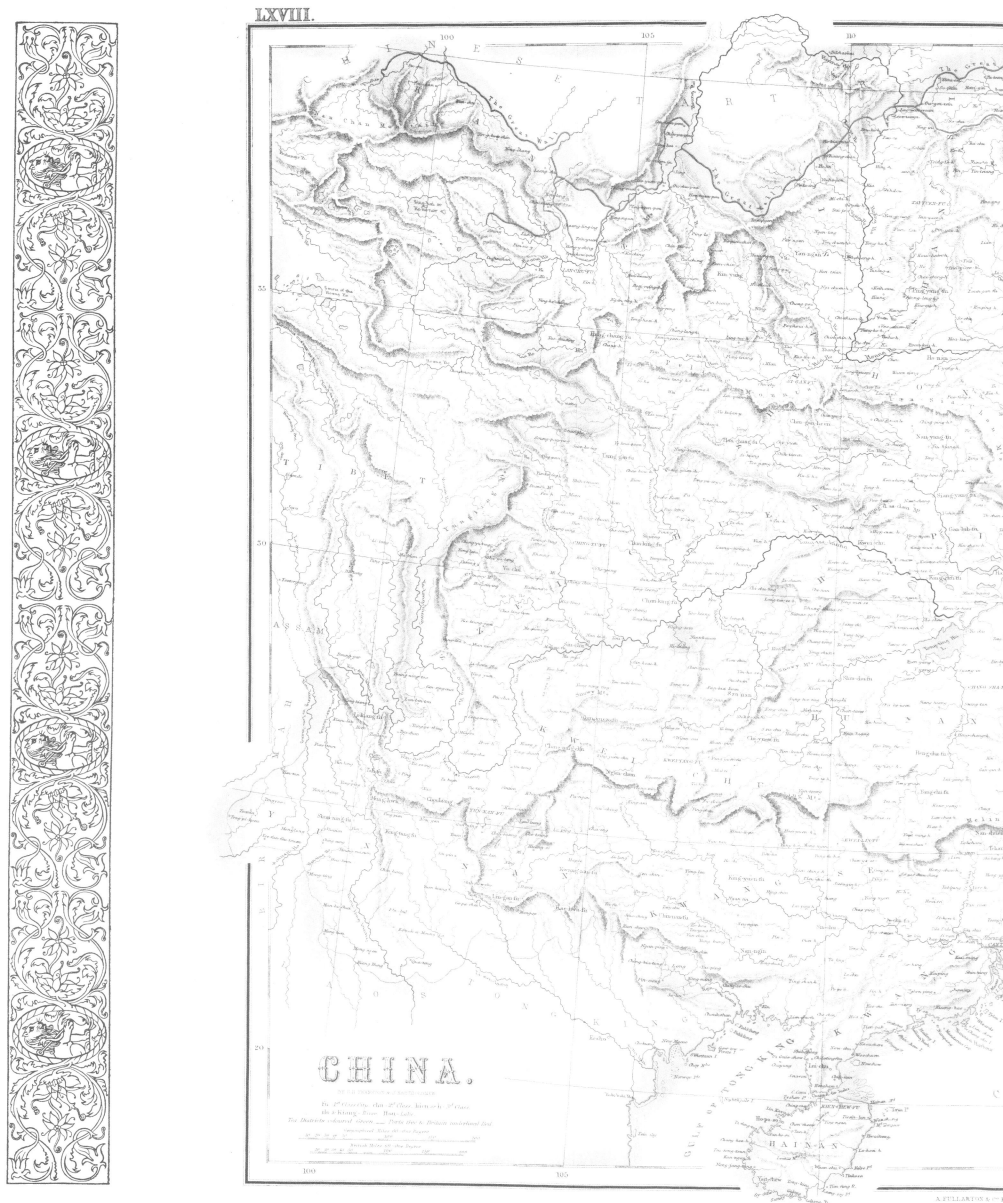

CHINA.

A. FULLARTON & C° E...